T0366201

A PRACTICAL GUIDE TO
BRAIN DATA
ANALYSIS

A PRACTICAL GUIDE TO
BRAIN DATA ANALYSIS

Armando Freitas da Rocha
Research on Artificial and Natural Intelligence (RANI), Brazil

Carlos Thomaz
Centro Universitário da FEI, Brazil

Fábio Theoto Rocha
Centro Universitário da FEI, Brazil

João Paulo Vieito
Polytechnic Institute of Viana do Castelo, Portugal

World Scientific

NEW JERSEY · LONDON · SINGAPORE · BEIJING · SHANGHAI · HONG KONG · TAIPEI · CHENNAI · TOKYO

Published by

World Scientific Publishing Co. Pte. Ltd.

5 Toh Tuck Link, Singapore 596224

USA office: 27 Warren Street, Suite 401-402, Hackensack, NJ 07601

UK office: 57 Shelton Street, Covent Garden, London WC2H 9HE

Library of Congress Cataloging-in-Publication Data

Names: Rocha, A. F. (Armando Freitas), 1946–   author. | Thomaz, Carlos, author. |
    Vieito, João Paulo, author.
Title: A practical guide to brain data analysis / Armando Freitas da Rocha
    (Research on Artificial and Natural Intelligence (RANI), Brazil), Carlos Thomaz
    (Centro Universitário da FEI, Brazil), Fábio Theoto Rocha (Centro Universitário da FEI, Brazil),
    João Paulo Vieito (Polytechnic Institute of Viana do Castelo, Portugal).
Description: New Jersey : World Scientific, 2016.
Identifiers: LCCN 2016032952 | ISBN 9789813144439 (hbk : alk. paper)
Subjects: LCSH: Decision making. | Neuroscience.
Classification: LCC BF448 .R64 2016 | DDC 153.8/3--dc23
LC record available at https://lccn.loc.gov/2016032952

British Library Cataloguing-in-Publication Data
A catalogue record for this book is available from the British Library.

Desk Editors: Herbert Moses/Alisha Nguyen

Typeset by Stallion Press
Email: enquiries@stallionpress.com

Printed in Singapore

Preface

In the last decades, several researchers from neurosciences and human and social sciences areas started to be interested in understanding how the human brain works on decision-making. This is actually one of the most interesting and challenging field of investigations in all social sciences. In addition, understanding about brain functioning was declared in the United States a priority concern, and the National Institute of Health (NIH)[1] recommend that this task shall involve multidisciplinary research and studies aiming to investigate human decision-making as much ecological as possible.

Several technologies are used to map the brain activity in humans: positron emission tomography (PET), single-photon emission computerized tomography (SPECT), functional magnetic resonance imaging (fMRI) and electroencephalography (EEG). PET and SPECT require use of positron-emitting molecules (tracer) that restrict their applications in human studies. fMRI and MEG demand high-cost equipment and special facilities that make implementation of ecological studies about human decision-making difficult. In addition, fMRI has a low temporal resolution although providing an excellent spatial discrimination of brain activity. EEG records electrical cortical activity at very speedy rates, but it has been criticized to have low spatial resolution and to be unable to sense subcortical activity. However, recent developments have improved significantly the EEG cortical spatial resolution.

The EEG portability makes its use very easy not only in human-friendly environments, but also in places where professional activities

---

[1] http://web.stanford.edu/class/symsys100/Report_BRAIN2025_AScientificVision.pdf.

are performed. Because of this, EEG was used here to record brain activity associated to financial decision-making in simulated trading conditions; moral dilemma judgment; vote decision one week before election day; and analysis of media propaganda broadcasted by TV and radio to influence voter decision.

Another NIH recommendation is the use of different statistical techniques, especially multivariate analysis, to study experimental data. Here, we use most of these techniques available for studying EEG recorded activity. This approach proved to be very fruitful and it permitted a very complex characterization of cerebral dynamics of decision-making.

Moreover, NIH has also recommended that data and results should be shared with scientific community. Data and results of the experiments described in this book are provided in four Excel books, called here EEG_Books, and are available for download at http://www.eina.com.br/software/. Results described and discussed especially in Chapters 7–9 are available at EEG_StockMarket, EEG_Dilemma, EEG_Vote and EEG_Marketing. Readers may check all these contents and discussions by simply controlling only three sets of variables: cortical area selection, time window range and statistical significant threshold.

Another helpful use of the EEG_Books is related to teaching decision-making in the different graduate and undergraduate courses. Teachers may create, for instance, exercises that demand handling the above control variables to study cortical activation associated to several topics discussed in this book or any other question he/she may find interesting or appropriate.

In short, this book aims to be a practical guide for undergraduate and graduate students, teachers and researchers from the different areas of science interested in studying and discussing human decision-making not only focusing on specific subject, but also on topics. In fact, the book may have different reading strategies, because each chapter has been written to be as self-contained as possible even if this approach required some pieces of information to be redundantly repeated along the book. Therefore, as suggestion, readers from different areas may choose, at least for the first reading, the most interesting chapter from their point of view.

To accomplish this achievement, the book is organized as follows:

Chapter 1 provides an overview of the literature on neuroeconomics and neurofinances; focuses attention on brain activity associated to dilemma judgment and ends summarizing our results on experiments in the interface between neurosciences, politics and marketing.

Chapter 2 presents and discusses the neuroeconomic model for decision-making previous published by some of the authors. It is composed of the following sections: reasoning process, financial and economics decision-making. To propose formal models to discuss decision-making is another NIH recommendation.

Chapter 3 describes brain organization from cellular to macrocircuit point of view, stressing the distributed character of brain processing associated to decision-making. It is composed of the following sections: the neuron, the cortex, the basic structure of the cortex: the cortical column, the distributed character of cortical processing, the properties of distributed intelligent processing systems and neural networks.

Chapter 4 introduces and describes many classical neural circuits involved in value, benefit and risk evaluation; working memory; attention control; memory access; arithmetic calculations; language processing and production; acting and hypothesizing about others intention.

Chapter 5 presents and illustrates the different techniques available for mapping brain activity in humans and briefly describes and illustrates all techniques employed in Chapters 7–9.

Chapter 6 discusses in details how to design a decision-making experiment using EEG to record brain activity and how the different statistical techniques are used to analyze obtained experimental data.

Chapter 7 focuses attention on experiments on financial decision-making associated to a simulated stock trading.

Chapter 8 focuses attention on experiments on dilemma judgment.

Chapter 9 focuses attention on experiments on vote decision and media propaganda analysis.

Chapter 10 provides the theoretical ground for multivariate statistical analysis used in the present book, such as factor analysis (FA) and linear discriminant analysis (LDA), and it is intended to complement information discussed in Chapter 5 to the expert reader.

Chapter 11 focuses attention on some general properties of the neural circuits involved in the different types of decision-making discussed in Chapters 7–9.

Finally, Chapters 3 and 4 provide an overview of brain physiology and Chapter 5 describes all techniques that will be used in Chapters 7–9. These chapters compose a core reading for all types of readers.

We are in debt to all people in Brazil, Portugal and the Netherlands that volunteered to the experiments described here. We are very grateful to them because we have learned much about neural activity associated to decision-making from the EEG they allowed us to record. Also, we appreciated too the partnership, in many of the papers cited, here, of Eduardo Massad, Rachel A.J. Pownal, Marcelo N. Burattini, Roberto I.R. Lima and others.

About the Authors

 **Armando Freitas da Rocha** received his MD in 1970 from the School of Medicine of São Paulo, University of São Paulo, and his PhD in neurosciences in 1972 from the Institute of Biology, University of Campinas. His present interest is on interdisciplinary frontiers between neurosciences and social sciences, that is, neuroeconomy, neurofinances, neuromarketing, neuropolitics, neuroeducation, etc. His research employs EEG brain mapping and LORETA analysis to disclose the neural circuits involved in decision-making, learning, problem understanding and solving. There are people from different areas and from different countries involved in these researches. He authored or coauthored the books: *Neural Nets: A Theory for Brains and Machines* (Springer, 1992); Rocha, A.F., Massad, E., Pereira, A., Jr: *The Brain: From Fuzzy Arithmetic To Quantum Computing* (Springer, 2004) and *Neuroeconomics and Decision Making* (in Portuguese, LTC, Brazil, 2011). He published more than 100 papers.

Carlos Thomaz is Professor of Statistical Pattern Recognition at the Department of Electrical Engineering, Centro Universitario da FEI (FEI), Sao Paulo, Brazil. He is also a CNPq (Brazilian National Council for Scientific and Technological Development) Research Fellow and head of the Image Processing Lab funded by FAPESP (State of Sao Paulo Research Foundation) at FEI. In 1993, he received his BSc degree in electronic engineering from Pontifical Catholic University of Rio de Janeiro (PUC-Rio), Rio de Janeiro, Brazil. After working for six years in industry, he obtained the MSc degree in electrical engineering from PUC-Rio in 1999. In October 2000, he joined the Department of Computing at Imperial College London where he obtained the PhD degree in statistical pattern recognition in 2004. He was a Research Associate at the Department of Computing, Imperial College London, from December 2003 to January 2005 working in the UK EPSRC e-science project called Information eXtraction from Images (IXI). In 2012, he was awarded a University of Nottingham Brazil Visiting Fellowship to work in the Sir Peter Mansfield Magnetic Resonance Center from middle April to the first week of July. His general interests are in statistical pattern recognition, computer vision, medical image computing and machine learning, whereas his specific research interests are in limited-sample-size problems in pattern recognition.

Fábio Theoto Rocha is graduated in linguistic and obtained his PhD in neuroscience from the School of Medicine of the University of São Paulo. Now he is a researcher at the Department of Electrical Engineering in University Center, studying electroencephalographic signals to create brain mappings while volunteers solve different kinds of cognitive tasks. His main interests are in language learning and decision-making. He is also a consultant in the Institute for Research on Technology and Innovation, working in neuroscience and education, for the development of new educational technologies.

 **João Paulo Vieito** is Professor of Finance, and Director of the School of Business Studies at Polytechnic Institute of Viana do Castelo, Portugal. He received his PhD in Business Science, Finance Specialization, from the Faculty of Economics and Management, University of Porto. He also has an MSc in finance from Portuguese Catholic University and an MBA in Operations Management from Portuguese Catholic University and a degree in Management from ISCTE.

His research interests, on which he has published several papers in finance and economics journals, are in neurofinance corporate governance and market efficiency. He has been on the editorial board of journals like *Annals of Financial Economics, Journal of Modern Accounting and Auditing, Montenegro Economic Journal* and *Mudra Journal of Finance and Accounting*. He published in journals like *Corporate Governance an International Review, Journal of Behavioral Finance, Applied Economic Letters, International Review of Economic and Finance, Journal of Economic and Business, Journal of Economic and Finance, Quarterly Journal of Finance and Economics*, among several others.

He is a Program Director of the Post-Graduation in Finance and Banking at ESCE-IPVC. He has taught extensively in various MSc and MBAs. He was also presenter, chairman and discussant in numerous sessions in international, national and regional associations' meetings and symposia. Professor Vieito is also a member of Western Finance Association, Financial Management Association, Midwest Finance Association, Southern Finance Association and Eastern Finance Associations.

Contents

Chapter 1

Introduction

In this chapter, we provide a literature overview of research activities in frontiers between neurosciences and economy, finances, philosophy, politics and marketing with the aim of helping the reader to understand what has already been done in these interdisciplinary research frontiers. From this point of view, it is not an extensive literature review, because it is influenced by predominance of research on economy and finances and by a more academic discussion in other areas of social sciences. Information provided here is intended essentially to provide the literature background required to support the understanding of the subsequent chapters.

1.1 Economy and Finances

The use of neuroscience technologies to analyze how the brain makes financial decisions is very recent. One of the first investigations that join neuroscience and finance was done by Gehring and Willoughby (2002). These authors used electroencephalogram (EEG) to record brain activity associated with a financial game playing. They found that a negative component of event-related brain potential peaking around 265 ms, and probably generated by the anterior cingulated cortex, was greater in amplitude when a participant's choice between two alternatives resulted in a loss than when it resulted in a gain. Some years later, Kuhnen and Knutson (2005) found that nucleus accumbens is activated before people make risky decisions as well as risk-seeking mistakes, whereas the anterior insula area is activated before risk-less choices as well as risk-aversion mistakes. Another interesting find of these authors is that a positive emotional state induces people to take risk and be confident to evaluate investment options, and negative emotions like anxiety reduce the propensity to take risk (Kuhnen and Knutson, 2011). Paulus *et al.* (2002) and Paulus and Frank (2006) showed that prefrontal cortex and anterior cingulated cortex modulate nonlinear decision weight function of uncertain prospects.

Other studies have added more information to the understanding of the process of financial decision, showing that it involves the participation of orbitofrontal cortex, medial prefrontal cortex (MPFC), amygdala, nucleus accumbens and many other neural structures (e.g., Bland and Schaefer, 2011; Burgess *et al.*, 2011; Breiter *et al.*, 2001; Cohen *et al.*, 2007, 2008; Davis *et al.*, 2011; FitzGerald *et al.*, Gehring and Willoughby, 2002; Knutson *et al.*, 2003, 2005; Kuhnen and Knutson, 2005; Knutson and Bossaerts, 2007; Knutson, 2005; McClure *et al.*, 2004; Preuschoff *et al.*, 2006a,b; Samanez-Larkin *et al.*, 2010; Tobler *et al.*, 2007). Based on these results, Rocha and Rocha (2011) and Rocha (2013) proposed that various neural circuits are recruited to handle the many tasks required by financial decision-making, such as aversion, risk and benefit assessments and analyses of many other variables such as stock price, portfolio value evolution, market volatility, etc. This distributed character of neural financial processing has also been reported in recent literature (e.g., Bartra *et al.*, 2013; Minati *et al.*, 2012a,b).

Although EEG has been used to study brain correlates of financial decision-making (Bland and Schaefer, 2011; Cohen *et al.*, 2007, 2008; Davis *et al.*, 2011; Gehring and Willoughby, 2002), Functional Magnetic Resonance Imaging (fMRI) has been the tool of choice to investigate decision-making (e.g., Burgess *et al.*, 2011; Breiter *et al.*, 2001; Frydman *et al.*, 2010; Huetell *et al.*, 2006; Kerstin *et al.*, 2006; Knutson *et al.*, 2003, 2005; Kuhnen and Knutson, 2005; Knutson and Bossaerts, 2007; Knutson, 2007; McClure *et al.*, 2004, 2005, 2006; Polezzi *et al.*, 2010; Preuschoff *et al.*, 2006a,b; Samanez-Larkin *et al.*, 2010; Seymour *et al.*, 2008; Tobler *et al.*, 2007).

fMRI has high spatial discriminative power but very poor temporal resolution. In addition, event-related fMRI protocols generally allow for the study of brain activity following but not preceding events of interest like decision-making events and are not suitable for studying tasks of variable duration like financial decision-making. Moreover, fMRI studies require experiments to be done in a very unnatural and unfriendly environment, for example, a hospital or research facility. In contrast, EEG has high temporal resolution, and event-related techniques are flexible enough to allow both backward and forward analyses concerning events of interest as well as studies of tasks of variable duration. However, EEG records electrical activity generated only by cortical neurons. Recently, developments improved EEG spatial resolution (Pascual-Marqui, 2002; Pascual-Marqui *et al.*, 2002) permitting identification of the many different sets of neurons enrolled in complex reasoning (e.g., Rocha *et al.*, 2011, 2015). Other techniques such as quantification of the amount of information ($H(e_i)$) provided by the distinct electrodes about tasks being processed and factor analysis of such information may be used to disclose the patterns of activity associated with the different neural circuits enrolled in financial decision-making. In addition, EEG equipment is portable and allows for experiments to be done in more ecological environments. Because of this, Rocha *et al.* (2013a,b,c, 2015) proposed EEG as an adequate tool for analysis of brain activity associated with decision-making whenever focus is not on subcortical structures.

Neuroeconomics and neurofinance propose that investors are not always rational in their financial decisions (e.g., Kuhnen and Knutson, 2005; Huettel *et al.*, 2006; McClure *et al.*, 2004). In other words, they do not always try to maximize their profits (Sanfey *et al.*, 2003). In addition, Seymour and McClure (2008) show that people is extremely susceptible to manipulation of their expectations and evaluations of prices. They judge options and prices in relative terms rather than absolute ones and use them as anchored prices to make the decisions. If the difference between the prices of selling and buying is acceptable, then negotiation occurs, and the seller and the buyer may converge to a final closing price (Rocha and Rocha, 2011) but if selling and buying price difference is not acceptable, no trade occurs. Buying and selling prices are, therefore, anchored on the buying and selling closing prices of the preceding trades.

Literature in finance and neurosciences describes that, on average, women are more risk-averse than men when making financial decision investment (e.g., Vandegrift and Brown, 2005). Lee *et al.* (2009) analyzed gender effects on the process of risk-taking and found that activation in the right insula and bilateral orbitofrontal cortex is stronger in female than the male participants while they were performing in the risky-gain tasks. When taking the same level of risk relative to men, women tend to engage in more neural processing involving the insula and the bilateral orbitofrontal cortex to update and valuate possible uncertainty associated with risk-taking decision-making. Burgdorfa and Pankseppa (2006) and Xue *et al.* (2010) complement this information describing that insula is activated during the decision process, using past experiences to make future decisions.

Based on Iowa Card Task, Bolla *et al.* (2004) found that men and women activate different parts of the brain when solving the same decision-making task. Using the same test, Overman (2004) found that females tended to choose cards associated with immediate wins and males tended to choose cards related with long-term outcome, meaning that women prefer investments that produce short-term outcomes. Lighthall *et al.* (2012) complement this investigation describing that when stress level is manipulated, its impact on reward-related decision processing differs depending on the gender.

More recently, Vieito *et al.* (2015) used EEG technology to study financial decision in a simulated traded decision game and found that market volatility influences chosen trading strategies that enroll different neural circuits. Rocha *et al.* (2015) showed that males and females recruited different cortical areas to successfully play this game. Results from these studies are discussed in detail in Chapter 7.

1.2   Social Sciences

Evolution has shaped humans to live in society. This may generate conflicts of interest triggered competing personal and social needs.

Moral and law are aimed to offer solutions to solve or avoid these conflicts. They provide two distinct sets of rules or norms for such a purpose. Whenever rules are broken and wrong doing is established, punishment has to be provided and enforced to avoid future norm breaking. Wrongdoing is prevented by coercion. Moral enforcement is a matter for divine or community reproach, and therefore the degree of coercion of moral rules is low. In case of law, enforcement is the matter of justice and government. Justice is in charge of judging wrongdoing and prescribing punishment, while government is in charge of enforcing punishment (Hobes, 1651). The degree of law rule coercion depends on the degree of punishment and efficacy of enforcing. How norms are defined is another difference between moral and law. Moral rules born from the different values of the distinct groups living in a given society, therefore they are never universal in that society. Law rules, in contrast, are issued by legislative that is defined as representative for all different peoples forming a given society, therefore juridical norms are supposed to be universal for that society. The amount of freedom any individual in a given society enjoys is directly dependent on the efficiency of their moral and law norms of conduct. Thus, individual freedom depends more on culture and efficiency of State, as composed by legislative, justice and government, than on genetically inherited rights (Hegel, 1821).

Neurosciences start to disclose organization and properties of pleasure, pain and fear systems that are at the core of human emotions and signal how successful or not the individual is being in handling their goals. Experiments are showing that different neural systems are in charge of evaluating and handling pleasure associated with expected and experienced benefits in acting; in charge of evaluating and handling fear of risks or threatens in the expectancy of acting and in charge of evaluating and handling incurred pains. These neural systems are, therefore, in charge of evaluating benefits and risk in order to calculate action adequacy.[1] In addition,

---

[1] Bentham (1781) has introduced the concept of *action utility* as a measure that increases with benefits and decreases with risk promoted by its implementation. However, the word *utility* has nowadays many distinct meanings, most of them correlating action with only the expected or provided benefit, with no mention to risk. Because of this, the

neurosciences have discovered that benefit and risk are evaluated both from personal and social perspectives by different neural circuits. Rocha *et al.* (2009) named these two different neural systems, respectively, as personal (PES) and interpersonal (IES) evaluating systems. They also proposed that action acceptance increases with social benefit and decreases with personal risk, whereas social coercion increases with social risks and decreases with personal benefits. In this context, *willingness to act* is directly dependent on action acceptance and inversely dependent on social coercion.[2]

1.2.1   Moral

Moral and ethics are important issues in human societies and have been important subjects for discussion in the works of classical philosophers and continue to be interesting topics in current philosophical discussions. Recently, the development of new techniques for studying the human brain has brought moral and ethical discussions to the realm of neuroscience investigations and allowed researchers to study the brain dynamics of moral dilemma judgments (Greene *et al.*, 2001, 2004; Borg *et al.*, 2006; Moll and Oliveira Souza, 2007; Rocha *et al.*, 2013a,b).

Greene *et al.* (2001) used fMRI to study moral dilemma judgment of the type:

> The trolley dilemma: (F) A runaway trolley is headed for five people who will be killed if it proceeds on its present course. (A) The only way to save them is to hit a switch that will turn the trolley onto an alternate set of tracks where it will kill one person instead of five. (D) Is it appropriate to switch the tracks?
>
> The foot bridge dilemma: (F) Similar to the trolley dilemma, the trolley is on a path that will kill five people. (A) The five people could be saved if you push a stranger in front of the trolley; however, the stranger would be killed. (D) Is it appropriate to push the stranger?

Although the two dilemmas have the same logical structure, the judgments about these two dilemmas are claimed totally different.

---

word adequacy is preferred here, with a specific semantics that is formally defined as $\text{adequacy} = f\left(\text{benefit}, \frac{1}{\text{risk}}\right)$.

[2]This model is discussed in Chapter 2.

Subjects are uncertain about the trolley dilemma (named impersonal dilemma–ID) and choose to save the people on 50% of the time. In contrast, subjects are prone to reject to save the people approximately 70% of the time in the case of the foot bridge dilemma (named personal dilemma–PD).

Greene *et al.* (2001, 2004) proposed that enrollment of emotional neural circuits involving neurons at the MPFC, posterior cingulate cortex (PCC) and bilateral superior temporal sulcus (STS) would explain behavioral differences concerning PD and ID judgment, and they interpreted their "behavioral results as evidence that when participants responded in a utilitarian manner (judging personal moral violations to be acceptable when they serve a greater good) such responses not only reflected the involvement of abstract reasoning but also the engagement of cognitive control in order to overcome prepotent social-emotional responses elicited by these dilemmas".

Although the work of Greene *et al.* (2001, 2004) has been influential in the realm of psychology, their work has been criticized. For example, McGuire *et al.* (2009) claimed that only a small number of dilemmas used by Greene *et al.* (2001, 2004) drive the findings that PD and ID are correlated with dissociable neural systems. Michail (2007) argued that the distinction between PD and ID is overly crude and unable to explain the variability that is found in the responses to the trolley problems. Finally, Borg *et al.* (2006) criticized Greene *et al.* for using more emotive language in reference to family and friends in PD compared with ID and for ambiguously asking whether actions were "appropriate". Finally, other deontological principles have being proposed to guide the judgments of PDs and IDs (e.g., Borg *et al.*, 2006).

In a recent paper, Shenhav and Greene (2010) pointed out that moral decision involves, on the one side, trade-offs among costs and benefits of varying magnitude and, on the other side, uncertainty about outcomes that vary in their probability of occurrence. They proposed that complex life-and-death moral decisions that affect others depend on neural circuitry adapted for more basic, self-interested decision-making involving material rewards and risks. This recent interpretation of their investigations is in line with the neuroeconomic model for dilemma judgment proposed by Rocha *et al.* (2013a,b).

Utilitarianism is an ethical theory holding that the proper course of action is the one that maximizes the overall "happiness" and its origin has been traced to Bentham's proposal (1789) of the "greatest happiness principle", or the principle of utility. By "happiness", he understood a predominance of "pleasure" over "pain". In this context, the amount of happiness is to be proportional to the ratio pleasure/pain, and the amounts of pleasure and pain are obtained, in his view, by summing up all pleasure and pain triggered during the proper course of action. Rocha *et al.* (2009) equated pleasure with the feeling triggered by the benefits associate with the intended action, and equated pain, fear or displeasure with the feeling triggered by the risks associated with the intended action, to propose a neuroeconomic model to calculate the utility of the action. The probability of accepting the action as the solution of a task is dependent on its utility.

In this context, the utilitarian solution of a dilemma depends on the ratio between expected benefits and risks (Rocha *et al.*, 2013a,b). In the case of the trolley and foot bridge dilemma, the benefit is mostly determined by the pleasure of saving five people, while the risk is determined by both the displeasure of breaking the rule of *not killing unless in self-defense* and the probability of being unsuccessful in implementing the proposed action is determined by the difficulty of the task. Both the benefit of saving five people and the displeasure of killing one are the same for both PD and ID, but the difficulty of *pushing a stranger* is for sure greater than that of *hitting a switch*. Therefore, the utility of *saving five people* in the case of the footbridge dilemma is smaller than that in the case of the trolley dilemma. As a consequence, a smaller number of people will consider the action of *killing one person* as appropriate in PD case in comparison with ID case. The fact that the risk is not zero even in ID case explains why not all people decide to save the *five endangered people* in the case of the trolley dilemma. As a matter of fact, ID risk is high because 50% of people refuse to kill one to save five.

Taking into account the above discussion, it is possible to conclude that:

(a) moral judgment is sensitive to both social and personal risk in implementing the action proposed as solution dilemma,

(b) risk is dependent on both amount of harm and probability of its occurrence and

(c) willingness to implement the proposed action is dependent on a risk/benefit analysis.

Rocha *et al.* (2013a,b) recorded EEG while volunteers were solving the same dilemma used by Greene *et al.* (2001, 2004, 2010). Their results show that the dilemma judgment correlates well with the expected losses and it is associated with three different patterns of brain activity that are clearly different for accepting or rejecting the proposed solution. These patterns are proposed to disclose the neural circuits involved in benefit and risk evaluation, calculating intention to act and controlling decision-making. Regression analysis showed that activity at some cortical areas favor action implementation by increasing intention to act, while activity at some other areas oppose it by decreasing intention to act. LORETA analysis revealed the cortical areas enrolled by these neural circuits. These results are discussed in details in Chapter 8.

1.2.2 Law

The interdisciplinary field of science involving neurosciences and law has attracted attention of many scholars by distinct reasons, such as understanding and automatically detecting lies (e.g., Greenemeier, 2007), defining criminal responsibility (e.g., Aspinwall *et al.*, 2012; Klaming and Koops, 2012), methodological (e.g., Eagleman and Flores, 2012) and philosophical issues (e.g., Schleim, 2012), etc. However, it is necessary to keep in mind that despite its impressive development in the last half century, neurosciences lack strong, well-supported and formalized theories to guide experimental studies about complex cognitive tasks. This limits the impact any contribution of neurosciences to law may have in the near future (Rocha, 2013a).

First, it is necessary to investigate how, for example, positive law influences neural circuits involved in personal and social decision-making taking into consideration analysis of personal and social risks. Attention has to be devoted to investigate neural circuits involved in computing other's intentions in order to have a better understanding of criminal responsibility from neurosciences point of view. Studies on conscious versus unconscious decision-making are a must for the same purpose. This is just to cite some few important questions to guide future studies.

1.2.2.1 *Neurodynamics of a social decision-making*

Brazil carried out the Firearm Commerce Referendum calling for a collective decision about prohibiting the commerce of firearms with the purpose of reducing criminality. Voting is mandatory in Brazil, and political campaign takes advantage of radio/TV-free propaganda 40 days prior election. Two political alliances arouse in the Brazilian Congress to run the campaign for the *Yes* (in favor of firearm commerce prohibition) and *No* (against firearm commerce prohibition) vote. If *Yes* predominated over *No* voters in this referendum, a law prohibiting the commerce of firearms would be approved and included in Brazilian Justice Code.

The media campaign stressed the benefits and costs of the *Yes* and *No* vote, trying to oppose the benefits of one decision against the risks of the opposite one. Rocha *et al.* (2010) proposed that willingness or intention to vote *Yes* or *No* would depend on the evaluation of personal and social risks and benefits associated with each type of vote at both PES and IES. It was also assumed that *Yes* vote would be mostly influenced by the analysis carried at IES, whereas *No* vote would be mostly influenced by the analysis carried at PES.

The time constraints imposed by the necessity of studying a reasonable number of voters during a very short time (in the present case, five days before the election day) imposed EEG as the tool of choice for recording and analyzing the brain activity in a simulated election.

Factor analysis identifies, in general, three different patterns of brain activity explaining 80% of $H(e_i)$ covariation associated to vote decision. Rocha *et al.* (2009) proposed that these FA patterns disclosed three different types of neural circuits in decision-making (Ribas *et al.*, 2013; Rocha *et al.*, 2009):

(1) Pattern P_1 is proposed to disclose the activity of the neural circuits enrolled in recognizing the possible problem solutions and evaluating their associated risks and benefits.
(2) Pattern P_3 is proposed to disclose the activity of neural circuits in charge of calculating action adequacy, fairness and willingness taking into consideration the results calculated by P_1 neural networks.
(3) Pattern P_2 is proposed to disclose the activity of the executive neural systems in charge to trigger decision-making process and selecting the action to be implemented taking into consideration information provided by P_1 and P_3 neural networks.

Rocha *et al.* (2015) used different techniques to study the brain activity associated with a voter's perception of the truthfulness of media arguments and their influence on voting decisions. Their results clearly showed that vote decision was not influenced by arguments that were introduced by propaganda, which were typically driven by specific social or self-interest motives. However, different neural circuits were identified in the analysis of each type of propaganda argument, independent of the declared vote (for or against the control) intention.

All these results are discussed in details in Chapter 9.

1.2.2.2 *Future*

The understanding of the process of decision-making that may be provided by neurosciences certainly will be of great use not only in daily court activities, but also to help society to produce better juridical norms to increase liberty and happiness of their individuals. However, as stressed before, there is a lot of work to be done in order to achieve such goals.

One of the questions raised by the present work concerns about the need to formalize a sound set of concepts that are the core of law and justice to guide the experimental research required to understand their neural basis. It was assumed here that this kind of approach will provide important and useful information to support the hopes of this new interdisciplinary endeavor.

For such a purpose, the present work discusses and proposes some formal development for the concepts of action acceptance, coercion, adequacy and fairness, as well as of willingness to act (Chapter 2). To illustrate how supporting information for theoretical constructs may be obtained from experimental studies, the results of a social decision about a proposal for a juridical norm studied by Rocha *et al.* (2009) is presented and discussed (Chapter 9).

However, it is not claimed here that either the theoretical model or the experimental approach discussed are unique solutions for the questions that were raised. Instead, the main point in discussion is the necessity to join people from both neurosciences and law to design well-planned experimental studies that may contribute to the understanding of human decision-making and to the development of better justice systems in the future.

References

Aspinwall, L., Brown, T., Tabery, J. (2012). The double-edged sword: Does biomechanism increase or decrease judges' sentencing of psychopaths? *Science*, 337, 846–849.

Bartra, O., McGuire, J., Kable, J. (2013). The valuation system: A coordinate-based meta-analysis of BOLD fMRI experiments examining neural correlates of subjective value. *NeuroImage*, 76, 412–427.

Bentham, J. (1781). The principles of morals and legislation. In: *Great Books in Philosophy*. Prometheus Books, Amherst, NY.

Bentham, J. (1789). An introduction to the principles of morals and legislation. In: Appud, Bernestein, P.L. *Against the Gods*. Wiley, New York, p. 189.

Bland, A., Schaefer, A. (2011). Electrophysiological correlates of decision making under varying levels of uncertainty. *Brain Research*, 1417, 55–66.

Bolla, K., Eldreth, D., Matochik, J., Cadet, J. (2004). Sex-related differences in a gambling task and its neurological correlates. *Cerebral Cortex*, 14(11), 1226–1232.

Borg, J.S., Hynes, C., Van Horn, J., Grafton, S., Sinnott-Armstrong, W. (2006). Consequences, action, and intention as factors in moral judgments: An fMRI investigation. *Journal of Cognitive Neuroscience*, 18(5), 803–817.

Breiter, H., Aharon, I., Kahneman, D., Dale, A., Shizgal, P. (2001). Functional imaging of neural responses to expectancy and experience of monetary gains and losses. *Neuron*, 30, 619–639.

Burgdorfa, J., Pankseppa, J. (2006). The neurobiology of positive emotions. *Neuroscience and Biobehavioral Reviews*, 30, 173–187.

Burgess, P., Gonen-Yaacovi, G., Volle, E. (2011). Functional neuroimaging studies of prospective memory: What have we learnt so far? *Neuropsychologia*, 49, 2246–2257.

Cohen, M., Elger, C., Ranganat, C. (2007). Reward expectation modulates feedback-related negativity and EEG spectra. *NeuroImage*, 35, 968–978.

Cohen, M., Ridderinkhof, K., Haupt, S., Elger, C., Fell, J. (2008). Medial frontal cortex and response conflict: Evidence from human intracranial EEG and medial frontal cortex lesion. *Brain Research*, 1238(31), 127–142.

Davis, C., Hauf, J., Wu, D., Everhart, D. (2011). Brain function with complex decision making using electroencephalography. *International Journal of Psychophysiology*, 79, 175–183.

Eagleman, D., Flores, S. (2012). Defining a neurocompatibility index for criminal justice systems: A framework to align social policy with modern brain science. *Law of the Future Series*, 1, 161–172.

Gehring, W., Willoughby, J. (2002). The medial frontal cortex and the rapid processing of monetary gains and losses. *Science*, 295, 2279–2282.

Greene, J., Sommerville, R., Nystrom, L., Darley, J., Cohen, J. (2001). An fMRI investigation of emotional engagement in moral judgment. *Science*, 293, 2105–2108.

Greene, J., Nystrom, L., Nystrom, A., Engel, A., Darley, J., Cohen, J. (2004). The neural bases of cognitive conflict and control in moral judgment. *Neuron*, 44, 389–400.

Greenemeier, L. (2007). Are you a liar? Ask your brain. *Scientific American*. http://www.scientificamerican.com/article/lie-brain-fmri-polygraph/.

Hegel, G. (1821). *The Philosophy of History. Dover Philosophical Classics*. Dover Publications, Mineola, NY.

Hobbes, Thomas (1994 [1651/1668]) *Leviathan*. ed Edwin Curley Hackett, Indianapolis.

Huettel, S., Stowe, C., Gordon, E., Warner, B., Platt, M. (2006). Neural signatures of economic preferences for risk and ambiguity. *Neuron*, 49, 766–775.

Klaming, L., Koops, E.J. (2012). Neuroscientific evidence and criminal responsibility in the Netherlands. In: Spranger, T.M. (Ed.) *International Neurolaw: A Comparative Analysis*. Springer, Heidelberg, pp. 227–256.

Knutson, B. (2007). Anticipation of monetary gain but not loss in older adults. *Nature Neuroscience*, 10, 787–791.

Knutson, B., Bossaerts, P. (2007). Neural antecedents of financial decisions. *Journal of Neuroscience*, 27, 8174–8177.

Knutson, B., Fong, G., Bennett, S., Adams, C., Hommer, D. (2003). A region of mesial prefrontal cortex tracks monetarily rewarding outcomes: Characterization with rapid event-related FMRI. *Neuroimage*, 18, 263–272.

Knutson, B., Taylor, J., Kaufman, M., Peterson, R., Glover, G. (2005). Distributed neural representation of expected value. *Journal of Neuroscience*, 25, 4806–4812.

Knutson, B., Rick, G., Wimmer, E., Prelec, D., Loewenstein, G. (2005). Neural predictors of purchases. *Neuron*, 53, 147–156.

Kuhnen, C., Knutson, B. (2005). The neural basis of financial risk taking. *Neuron*, 47, 763–770.

Kuhnen, C., Knutson, B. (2011). The influence of affect on beliefs, preferences, and financial decisions. *Journal of Financial Quantitative Analysis*, 46, 605–626.

Lee, T., Chan, C., Leung, A., Fox, P., Gao, J. (2009). Sex-related differences in neural activity during risk taking: an fMRI study. *Cerebral Cortex*, 19(6), 1303–1312.

Lighthall, N., Sakaki, M., Vasunilashorn, S., Nga, L., Somayajula, S., Chen, E., Samii, N., Massad, E., Rocha, A. (2006). Ambiguous grammars and the chemical transactions of life. Part I: Environmental constraints of grammar ambiguity. *Kybernetes*, 35, 1414–1430.

Mather, M. (2012). Gender differences in reward-related decision processing under stress. *Social Cognitive Affective Neuroscience*, 4, 476–484.

McClure, E., Monk, C., Nelson, E., Zarahn, E., Leibenluft, E., Bilder, R., Charney, D., Ernst, M., Pine, D. (2004). A developmental examination of gender differences in brain engagement during evaluation of threat. *Biological Psychiatry*, 55(11), 1047–1055.

McGuire, J., Langdon, R., Coltheart, M., Mackenzie, C. (2009). A reanalysis of the personal/impersonal distinction in moral psychology research. *Journal of Experimental Social Psychology*, 45, 577–580.

Minati, L., Grisoli, M., Seth, K., Ritchley, H. (2012a). Decision-making under risk: A graph-based network analysis using functional MRI. *NeuroImage*, 60, 2191–2205.

Minati, L., Grisoli, M., Franceschetti, S., Epifani, F., Granvillano, A., Medford, N., Harrison, N., Piacentini, S., Critchley, H. (2012b). Neural signatures of economic parameters during decision-making: A functional MRI (fMRI), electroencephalography (EEG) and autonomic monitoring study. *Brain Topography*, 25, 7396.

Overman, W. (2004). Sex differences in early childhood: Adolescence and adulthood on cognitive tasks that rely on orbital prefrontal cortex. *Brain Cognition*, 55(1), 134–147.

Overman, W., Frassrand, K., Ansel, S., Trawalter, S., Bies, B., Redmond, A. (2004). Performance on the IOWA card task by adolescents and adults. *Neuropsychologia*, 42(13), 1838–1851.

Pascual-Marqui, R. (2002). Standardized low resolution brain electromagnetic tomography (sLORETA): Technical details. *Methods & Findings in Experimental & Clinical Pharmacology*, 24D, 5–12.

Pascual-Marqui, R., Esslen, M., Kochi, K., Lehmann, D. (2002). Functional imaging with low resolution brain electromagnetic tomography (LORETA): A review. *Methods & Findings in Experimental & Clinical Pharmacology*, 24C, 91–95.

Paulus, M.P., Frank, L.R. (2006). Anterior cingulate activity modulates nonlinear decision weight function of uncertain prospects. *NeuroImage*, 30, 668–677.

Paulus, M., Hozac, N., Frank, L., Brown, G. (2002). Error rate and outcome predictability affect neural activation in prefrontal cortex and anterior cingulated during decision-making. *NeuroImage*, 15, 836–846.

Preuschoff, K., Bossaerts, P., Quartz, S. (2006a). Neural differentiation of expected reward and risk in human subcortical structures. *Neuron*, 51, 381–390.

Preuschoff, K., Quartz, S., Bossaerts, P. (2006b). Human insula activation reflects risk prediction errors as well as risk. *The Journal of Neuroscience*, 28(11), 2745–2752.

Ribas, L., Rocha, F.N., Ortega, R., Rocha, A., Massad, A. (2013). Brain activity and medical diagnosis: an EEG study. *Law of the Future*, 1, 161–172.

Rocha, A. (1992). *Neural Nets: A Theory for Brains and Machine. Lecture Notes in Artificial Intelligence.* Springer, Heidelberg.

Rocha, A.F., Rocha, F.T. (2011) *Neuroeconomia e o Processo Decisório*. LTC., São Paulo (in Portuguese).

Rocha, A. (2013a). Toward a better understanding of the relationship between neurosciences and law. *Law & Neuroscience eJournal*, 4(11).

Rocha, A. (2013b). What we learn about global systemic risk with neurosciences. *Neuroeconomics eJournal Financial Crises eJournal*, 2(90). http://papers.ssrn.com/abstract=2316765.

Rocha, A.F., Massad, E., Pereira Jr., A. (2004). *The Brain: From Fuzzy Arithmetic to Quantum Computing.* Springer. ISBN: 3-540-21858-0.

Rocha, F.T., Rocha, A.F., Massad, E., Menezes, R. (2005). Brain mappings of the arithmetic processing in children and adults. *Cognitive Brain Research*, 22, 359–372.

Rocha, A., Burattini, M., Rocha, F., Massad, E. (2009). A neuroeconomic modeling of attention deficit and hyperactivity disorder. *Journal of Biological Systems*, 17, 597–621.

Rocha, A., Rocha, F., Burattini, M., Massad, E. (2010). Neurodynamics of an election. *Brain Research*, 1351, 198–211.

Rocha, A., Rocha, F., Massad, E. (2011). The brain as a distributed intelligent processing system: An EEG study. *PLoS ONE*, 6(3), e17355.

Rocha, A.F., Rocha, F.T., Massad, E. (2013a). Moral dilemma judgment: A neuroeconomic approach. *Cognitive Social Science eJournal*, 5(60). http://papers.ssrn.com/abstract=2314771.

Rocha, A.F., Rocha, F.T., Massad, E. (2013b). Moral dilemma judgment revisited: A LORETA analysis. *Journal of Behavioral and Brain Science.* doi: 10.4236/jbbs.2013.38066.

Rocha, A., Lima Filho, R., Costa, H., Lima, I. (2013c). The 2008 crisis from the neurofinance perspective: Investor humor and market sentiment. *International Finance eJournal.* http://papers.ssrn.com/abstract=2332200.

Rocha, A., Vieito, J., Massad, E., Rocha, F., Lima, R. (2015). Electroencephalography activity associated to investment decisions: Gender differences. *Journal of Behavioral and Brain Science,* 5, 203–211.

Samanez-Larkin, G., Kuhnen, C., Yoo, D., Knutson, B. (2010). Variability in nucleus accumbens activity mediates age-related suboptimal financial risk taking. *Journal of Neuroscience,* 30, 1426–1434.

Sanfey, A., Rilling, J., Aronson, J., Nystrom, L., Cohen, J. (2003). The neural basis of economic decision-making in the ultimatum game. *Science,* 200, 1755–2175.

Schleim, S. (2012). Brains in context in the neurolaw debate: The examples of free will and "dangerous" brains. *International Journal of Law and Psychiatry,* 35, 104–111.

Seymour, B., McClure, S. (2008). Anchors, scales and the relative coding of value in the brain. *Current Opinion in Neurobiology,* 18, 173–178.

Shenhav, A., Greene, J. (2010). Moral judgments recruit domain — General valuation mechanisms to integrate representations of probability and magnitude. *Neuron,* 67, 667–677.

Tobler, P., Fletcher, C., Bullmore, E., Schultz, W. (2007). Learning-related human brain activations reflecting individual finances. *Neuron,* 54, 167–175.

Vandegrift, D., Brown, P. (2005). Gender differences in the use of high-variance strategies in tournament competition. *Journal of Socio-Economics,* 34(6), 834–849.

Vieito, J., Rocha, A., Rocha, F. (2015). Brain activity of the investor's stock market financial decision. *Journal of Behavioral Finance,* 16, 1–11.

Xue, G., Lu, Z., Levin, I., Bechara, A. (2010). The impact of prior risk experiences on subsequent risky decision-making: The role of the insula. *NeuroImage,* 50, 709–716.

Chapter 2

Decision-making Process

Understanding how the human brain makes decisions in several contexts is one of the biggest challenges in science for the next decades or centuries. Because people make decisions all the time, it is very important to choosing the adequate questions to be investigated, what implies to clearly define the meaning of words such as *necessity, motivation, intention, purpose*, etc. Any research in the area needs first to clearly define the fundamental concepts involved in the understanding of free will, in order to search for their neural correlates.

Any living being has to use available resources to maintain its identity in space and time, meaning that they, as primordial goals, need to obtain the resources to synthesize their constituent chemicals, to obtain energy to support their chemical transactions and to create other similar living beings, in other words, to reproduce themselves (Rocha and Rocha, 2011; Rocha *et al.*, 2013). Goal achievement and maintenance create necessity for goods and services. Such necessities motivate the animals to act in order to obtain them. Decision-making about how to satisfy needs is, therefore, the key issue in living (Rocha and Rocha, 2011). As life complexity increases, other complementary goals are implemented to maintain individual identity. The complexity of motivations increases as life evolves on Earth and puts increasingly demands upon computation resources to support decision-making.

2.1   Reasoning Process

Each action has a cost, implies a risk and provides a benefit. The amount of benefit is the amount of services or goods provided by the implemented action compared to the amount required to satisfy the motivating necessity. This way, benefit is also dependent on motivation and therefore on individual's preferences and aversions. The amount of risk is dependent on both the possibility of failure in implementing the action and the amount of harm this implementation may cause to the individual. Failure possibility is inversely related to the individual skills. Harm is either physical or psychological. Risk is high if the possibility of failure and harm is high. The cost is the amount of resources required to implement the action. From the neuroscientific point of view, cost implies the amount of energy required for action implementation, which in turn is dependent on the individual's skills. In the case of humans, cost may also imply amount of money (wealth resources) if action is to *buy* goods or services.

During action planning, previous experiences (knowledge) are used to estimate expected cost, risk and benefit. If action is implemented, the incurred cost and risk as well as the obtained benefit are used to evaluate the success in getting the desired goods or services (Figure 2.1).

Emotional feelings are used to measure benefits, risks and costs. Pleasure is the coin of benefit; it increases with expected and experienced benefits. Fear encodes evaluated risk, whereas pain

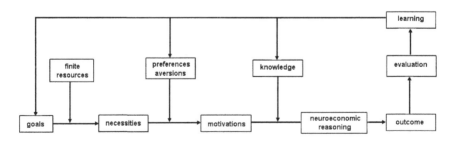

Figure 2.1   Deciding and learning (modified from Rocha *et al.*, 2013).

measures incurred risk. In general, people fear acting risky, although the amount of this fear varies among individuals. Pain measures incurred risk, and relief measures the avoided (not incurred) amount of expected risk. Tranquility and apprehension encode evaluated cost. Low cost inspires tranquility, whereas anxiety encodes high cost. Regret signals when incurred cost is high than the expected one, whereas proud signals the opposite.

The *willingness* of implementing a given action is mainly determined by the ratio (*risk/benefit*) between the expected benefit and risk of this action, whereas cost modulates this ratio, since high cost may reduce benefit and increase risk, whereas low cost may have the opposite effects. If benefit is high concerning risk, action implementation is highly possible. In contrast, if risk is high concerning benefit, action implementation has low possibility. Whenever the ratio (*risk/benefit*) approaches 1, conflict about action implementation increases and induces procrastination. In this context, Rocha and Rocha (2011) proposed that

$$P_a = \text{probability of acting,} \tag{2.1}$$

$$P_{na} = \text{probability of not acting,} \tag{2.2}$$

$$P_c = \text{procrastination,} \tag{2.3}$$

$$P_a + P_{na} + P_c = 1, \tag{2.4}$$

where P_a is the probability of acting, P_{na} the probability of not acting and P_c the procrastination.

If conflict is low, because either benefit or risk is high, procrastination tends to zero and hence

$$P_a + P_{na} \cong 1. \tag{2.5}$$

There is a rich neuroscience literature showing that benefit evaluation involves dopamine circuits (Berridge, 2003; Ernst *et al.*, 2004; van Gaalen *et al.*, 2006; Obayashi *et al.*, 2009; Panksepp, 1998), whereas risk assessment enrolls serotoninergic neurons (Graeff, 2003; Ledoux, 1996; Wright *et al.*, 2013), and cost evaluation is a subject for adrenergic circuits (Ledoux, 1996; Panksepp, 1998; Rocha and Rocha, 2011).

It is consensual in literature that orbitofrontal and medial prefrontal cortices are involved in preference encoding (Obayashi *et al.*, 2009); Amigdala is a key structure in fear assessment (Ledoux, 1996; O'Doherty *et al.*, 2001; Panksepp, 1998); Insula has an important role in aversion and risk assessment (Ledoux, 1996; O'Doherty *et al.*, 2001; Panksepp, 1998; Paulus *et al.*, 2002), and nucleus accumbens is a key structure in handling reward prediction and assessment (Ernst *et al.*, 2004; Obayashi *et al.*, 2009; O'Doherty *et al.*, 2001; Panksepp, 1998). Finally, it was proposed that calculation of both intention and probability of acting enrolls neurons located in parietal areas (Glimcher and Rustichini, 2004; Wright *et al.*, 2013).

Once action is implemented, the outcome is evaluated. This evaluation guides learning that may modify preferences or aversions as well as knowledge used to map necessities into motivation (Figure 2.1). Pleasant outcomes reinforce knowledge that maps necessity into the implemented actions, whereas unpleasant outcomes contribute to reinforce mapping of necessity to alternative actions other than the implemented one. Pleasant outcomes increase preferences and reduce aversions; unpleasant outcomes do the opposite. Because learning may change preferences, it may result in changing the goals.

Although initially influenced by their genetic patterns, people learn from living and adjust their goals and knowledge of how to satisfy their necessities in order to better adapt themselves to their living environment. The degree of success of this adaptation determines the degree of happiness/unhappiness of each individual. The capacity to adapt their goals to the available resources is the key of a happy life. But because people have different inheritances and experience different learning, they have different capacities of balancing necessities and available resources. In summary, different people make different decisions because they have different goals and therefore motivated lives.

It has been shown that neurons in several areas of the brain evaluate experienced benefit concerning the expected one, having their activity increased if experience exceeds expected benefit or decreased in the opposite case (Bayer and Glimcher, 2005; Rocha, 1997; Rocha *et al.*, 1998). Activity in these circuits remains the same if experience matches expected benefit. Learning occurs according to these evaluations, being the preferences, aversions and knowledge updated accordingly. In the same way, other neural circuits are in charge of monitoring risks and costs and promoting the required adjustment of preferences, aversions and knowledge. Learning, therefore, makes motivation to vary during the individual life time.

2.2   Financial and Economics Decision-making

Traditional finance theories assume that markets whose prices reflect all the available information are deemed to be efficient (Fama, 1970) and that betting on one sole strategy is riskier than diversification (Markowitz, 1952). Prices must have a random walk and thus must also be unpredictable. Because of this, rational agents do not achieve higher returns *ad infinitum* above average market returns on a risk-adjusted basis.

In contrast to traditional finance theories, neurofinance considers that investors are not always rational in their financial decisions (Kuhnen and Knutson, 2005). In other words, they do not always try to maximize their profits (Sanfey *et al.*, 2003). Emotional influence on decision-making has been proposed to explain the irrationality of the investor's decision (Camerer and Loewenstein, 2004; Rocha and Rocha, 2011).

Two aspects of future thinking influence decision-making (McClure *et al.*, 2004). The first is how steeply rewards are devalued as their delivery is pushed into the future, a phenomenon known as temporal discounting, and the second is the perceived dimension of future time, sometimes labeled "future time perspective". Although these two aspects of future thinking seem similar, they are not equivalent. Future time perspective measures a spontaneously chosen time period, which would not necessarily affect the way a person evaluates an event at a specific time in the future when explicitly cued to do so. Similarly, the rate at which reward decays across a specified delay may differ across individuals, even if they have a similar future time perspective (Fellow and Farah, 2005).

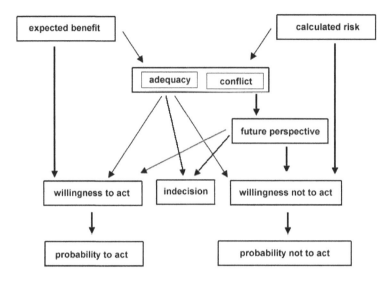

Figure 2.2   The neuroeconomic model for decision-making as proposed by Rocha *et al.* (2009, 2011, 2013).

Based on knowledge provided by neurosciences, Rocha *et al.* (2009, 2011, 2013) proposed a neuroeconomic-based decision-making model (Figure 2.2) that is dependent on the evaluation of expected rewards and risks assessed, simultaneously, in two decision spaces: the personal decision space (PDS) and the interpersonal decision space (IDS). Motivation to act is triggered by necessities to achieve and maintain primordial and complementary goals.

The *adequacy* of an action — for instance, selling or buying a stock — to fulfill a given necessity (e.g., saving money for retiring) is assumed to be dependent on the expected *reward* and *risk* that are evaluated in both the PDS (savings for oneself) and the IDS (savings for the family).

Conflict generated by expected reward and risk influences the *ease* (cognitive effort) and the future perspective of the decision-making (short-term versus long-term investment). Finally, the *willingness to act* (sell or buy stock) and *willingness not to act* (or holding the stock) within a *future perspective* are proposed to be the function of the expected *reward* and *risk* associated with the stock, as well as of the *adequacy* and *ease* of decision-making regarding selling or buying the stock. In this context, *willingness to act* increases as expected *benefit* augments in respect to calculated *risk*. In the same line of reasoning, *willingness not to act* increases as calculated *risk* augments in respect to expected *benefit*. Indecision in deciding is determined by the amount of conflict.

In a recent review of economic decision-making, Seymour and McClure (2008) show that people are extremely susceptible to manipulation of their expectations and evaluations of prices. People judge options and prices in relative, rather than absolute, terms and they use them as anchored prices. The value of the stock is dependent on the buying and selling-price offers. If the difference between these prices is acceptable, the negotiation occurs, and the seller and the buyer may converge to a final trading price (Rocha and Rocha, 2011). In contrast, if selling and buying price difference is not acceptable, no trade occurs. Buying and selling prices are, in turn, anchored on the closing prices of the preceding trades (Rocha and Rocha, 2011).

Anchored prices are noisy but trendy. Prices p_d on trading day d are equal to the prices p_{d-1} at day $d - 1$ plus an amount Δ_d of money, which is dependent on the difference between the buying and selling-price offers (Rocha and Rocha, 2011). They are noisy because Δ_d is noisy. The mean $\bar{\Delta}_{d,d+k}$ value of Δ_d for the interval of k days determines the price trend and will be positive for the bull market, negative for the bear market and null for a stationary market.

Anchored prices contain most of, but not all, the information investors need because they are trendy and noisy, as well as because Δ_d is not only dependent on the difference between the buying and selling price, but also on the market's humor (Rocha and Rocha, 2011). This humor, in turn, is dependent on the conflict associated with the benefit and risk estimation, as well as on price volatility that determines the strength of the anchoring process. If humor is greater than a given threshold ζ_d, then Δ_d is negative; otherwise, it is positive. External forces may change the actual value of ζ_d, which is influenced by media news, government decisions, national and international events, contagion, among other forces (Rocha and Rocha, 2011; Rocha *et al.*, 2013).

No matter how investors calculate expected benefits and risks, it may be proposed that risk and benefits are scaled in a nonlinear way to buying and selling prices. Because of this, Rocha and Rocha (2011) proposed that

$$\text{Perceived benefits} = f(\Delta^{s_i}) \qquad (2.6)$$

and

$$\text{Perceived risks} = f(\Delta^{s_i}) \qquad (2.7)$$

are the neural currency used in financial decision-making and are calculated from different points of view (selling or buying). However, if trade occurs, both the seller and the buyer converge to similar selling and buying prices even if having different selling-price disagreement perceptions due to their opposite benefit and risk perceptions.

Conflict in deciding about trading a stock is low irrespective of whether perceived benefit or risk is low or high. In contrast, conflict is high if the ratio risk/benefit approaches 1. In this line of reasoning,

$$\text{Conflict} = \omega_c * \text{Benefit} * \text{Risk}, \quad 0 < \omega_c < 4 \qquad (2.8)$$

such that conflict decreases as benefit or risk approximates zero and tends toward $\omega_c/4$ if the risk/benefit ratio approaches 1. In this context, conflict has values varying from 0 to $\omega_c/4$ ($0 \leq \text{Conflict} < 1$), and the actual value of ω_c determines how the individual evaluates stress. High values of ω_c characterize people that are stress-prone and low values of ω_c characterize people that are stress-resistant.

Besides conflict, volatility is also an important determinant of market humor (Rocha and Rocha, 2011). In this context, acceptable price variation (apv(d)) is proposed to be positive if market humor is above a given humor threshold and to be negative otherwise. In other words,

$$\text{Total conflict} = f(\text{Conflict, Volatility}), \qquad (2.9)$$
$$\text{Humor}(d) = \text{Humor threshold} - \text{Total conflict} \qquad (2.10)$$

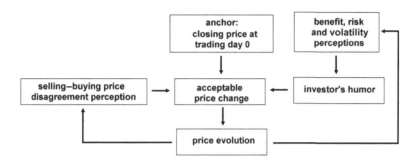

Figure 2.3 Establishing prices at the stock market as proposed by Rocha *et al.* (2011, 2013).

and

$$\mathrm{apv} = f(p(d), \mathrm{humor}(d)) \qquad (2.11)$$

such that acceptable trading prices p_d on trading day d is defined as

$$p_d = p_d + \mathrm{apv}. \qquad (2.12)$$

In these conditions, stock price evolution and the stock market index may be modeled as depicted in Figure 2.3. Given the closing price at the trading day 0, the selling and buying offers difference, the expected benefit and risk and the acceptable price variation for the next trade is estimated and price evolution is calculated.

References

Bayer, H., Glimcher, P. (2005). Midbrain dopamine neurons encode a quantitative reward prediction error signal. *Neuron*, 47, 129–141.

Berridge, K. (2003). Pleasures of the brain. *Brain and Cognition*, 52, 106–128.

Camerer, C., Loewenstein, G. (2004). Behavioral economics: Past, present, future. In: Camerer, C., Loewenstein, G., Rabin, M. (Eds.) *Advances in Behavioral Economics*. Princeton University Press, Princeton, NJ, pp. 3–52.

Ernst, M., Nelson, E., McClure, E., Monk, C., Munson, S., Eshel, N., Zarahn, E., Leibenluft, E., Zametkin, A., Towbin, K., Blair, J., Charney, D., Pine, D. (2004). Choice selection and reward anticipation: An fMRI study. *Neuropsychologia*, 42, 1585–1597.

Fama, E. (1970). Efficient capital markets: A review of theory and empirical work. *Journal of Finance* 25(2), 389–413.

Fellow, L., Farah, M. (2005). Different underlying impairments in decision-making following ventromedial and dorsolateral frontal lobe damage in humans. *Cerebral Cortex*, 15, 58–63.

Glimcher, P., Rustichini, A. (2004). Neuroeconomics: The consilience of brain and decision. *Science*, 306, 447–452.

Graeff, F. (2003). Serotonin, the periaqueductal gray and panic. *Neuroscience and Biobehaviorial*, 28, 239–259.

Kuhnen, C., Knutson, B. (2005). The neural basis of financial risk taking. *Neuron*, 47(5), 763–770.

Ledoux, J. (1996). *The Emotional Brain: The Mysterious Underpinning of Emotional Life*. Simon & Schuster, New York.

Markowitz, H. (1952). Portfolio selection. *Journal of Finance*, 7(1), 77–78.

McClure, S., Laibson, D., Lowenstein, G., Dochen, J. (2004). Separate neural systems value immediate and delayed monetary rewards. *Science*, 306, 503–507.

Obayashi, S., Nagai, Y., Suhara, T., Okauchi, T., Inaji, M., Iriki, A., Maeda, J. (2009). Monkey brain activity modulated by reward preferences: A positron emission tomography study. *Neuroscience Research*, 64, 421–442.

Rocha, A. F., Burattini, M. N., Rocha, F. R., Massad, E. (2009). A neuroeconomic modeling of attention deficit and hyperactivity disorder. *Journal of Biological Systems*, 17, 597–621.

Rocha, A. F., Rocha, F. T. (2011). *Neuroeconomia e o Processo Decisório*. LTC., São Paulo, Brazil (in Portuguese).

Rocha, A. F., Lima Filho, R. I. R., Costa, H. A. X., Lima, I. R. (2013). The 2008 crisis from the neurofinance perspective: Investor humor and market sentiment. *Economics of Networks eJournal* 5(74).

Sanfey, A., Rilling, J., Aronson, J., Nystron, L., Cohen, J. (2003). The neural basis of economic decision-making in the ultimatum game. *Science*, 300, 1755–1758.

Seymour, B., McClure, S. (2008). Anchors, scales and the relative coding of value in the brain, Current. *Opinion in Neurobiology*, 18, 173–178.

Chapter 3

How the Brain is Organized

This chapter describes what neuroscience knows, until the moment, about brain areas and functions.

3.1 The Neuron

The neuron is the major brain-processing unit (Figure 3.1). It is composed by a cell body containing its nucleus, where information about neuronal physiology is encoded into DNA, by axon (long cable) in charge of transmitting information encoded in its electrical activity to other neurons located in other areas of the brain, and dendrites that are short cellular ramifications in charge of receiving information transmitted by axons of neurons in other brain areas (Figure 3.1). Connections between neurons are established among pre-synaptic terminals, and dendrites.

Since the classical Galvani's experiments, electrical membrane gradients and their induced variations play an important role in the understanding of the cerebral physiology. These electrical membrane gradients are created by keeping a high concentration of sodium (Na) inside the cell and of potassium (K) at the outside cellular space. The Nobel prized work of Hodgkin and Huxley in the first half of the 20th century clearly identified the main membrane components governing its electrical behavior and formalized this behavior as equivalent to that of a dynamic system having two stable and one unstable equilibrium states (for further discussion of this subject, see Rocha, 1992).

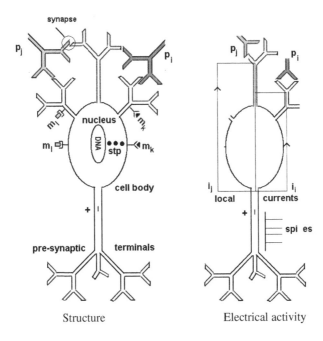

| Structure | Electrical activity |

Figure 3.1   The neuron.

Modifications of the permeability of Na and/or K at the dendrites allow these ions to move out (EPSP) or in (IPSP) the cell generate ionic currents that reach the axon where they may promote spike triggering that travels toward the presynaptic terminals if the resultant depolarization reaches a threshold level.[1] Spikes are instantaneous reversion of membrane potential with the inside of the neuron becoming positive to the external cellular space due to massive movements of Na ions toward the intracellular space. This is quickly followed by movements of K ions toward the extracellular space, recovering the normal state of the inside of the cell being negative in relation to the extracellular space. Spike frequency is determined by the intensity of local ionic currents. Spikes at the presynaptic terminals trigger the release of molecules, called transmitters, toward the extracellular to

---

[1]See, for example, animation about cellular electrical activity, e.g., http://highered.mhe ducation.com/sites/0072495855/student_view0/chapter14/animation_the_nerve_impulse. html.

bind to the dendrites of the next neuron promoting modifications of the permeability of Na and/or K.

Local responses (EPSP or IPSP) are generated by spike trains arriving by presynaptic axon terminals that trigger transmitter release that changes ionic permeability at the dendrites (Figure 3.1). Local responses are long-lasting to presynaptic spikes, because their time evolution depends on the dynamics of the activated ionic gates. Because of this, local responses retain some *memory* of the presynaptic activity.

Recently, brain scientists start to report that attachment of special molecules, called neuromodulators (m_l, m_k), to specific receptors located at dendrites and cell body triggers a sequence of molecular activations (stp in Figure 3.1) that influences DNA reading at the nucleus (for further information on this subject, see Rocha *et al.*, 1998). These experiments show how brain activity may control DNA reading that, in turn, may modify neuronal physiology to adapt it to best fit the survival of the animal in a given environment. These studies are disclosing the mechanisms of learning.

3.2 The Brain

The number of neurons in human brain varies from 76 (female) to 92 (male) billion, 20% of them composing the cortex and the remaining being distributed in many different subcortical structures (Figure 3.2). The cortex is divided into frontal, parietal, temporal and occipital lobes. Among subcortical structures, striatum and nucleus accumbens are frequently reported to be associated with financial decision-making, reward evaluation, etc.

The cortex is divided into motor cortex responsible for fine and complex control of muscles; sensory cortex receiving information from different types of sensory receptors and named according to the function of these receptors and the associative cortex that functions as an interface between the sensory and motor cortices.

Korbian Brodmann studied the histological structure of the human brain and divided the cortex into 52 different areas concerning the cytoarchitectonic characteristics. These areas are usually referred by their numbers as BA 1, 2, etc. in the present book.

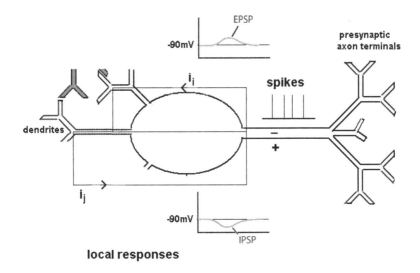

local responses

Figure 3.2   The human brain and Brodmann areas.

3.3   The Basic Structure of the Cortex: The Cortical Column

Despite the diversity of the cortical cytoarchitectonics, neurons in the cortex are organized into functional units, called cortical columns, that are disposed perpendicular to the brain surface in a parallel organization (Figure 3.3). Column's radius has a magnitude in the range of microns, and each column is composed of hundreds of neurons, but the number of other cells giving support to columnar activity is large than the number of neurons. The number of columns in the cortex is estimated to above 100 million units. Neurons inside each column operate as a processing unit, and nearby columns may have their activity synchronized increasing the number of neurons enrolled in a given cortical processing.

3.4   The Distributed Character of Cortical Processing

Cortical columns located at the different Brodmann areas become specialized in different types of cortical processing depending on their

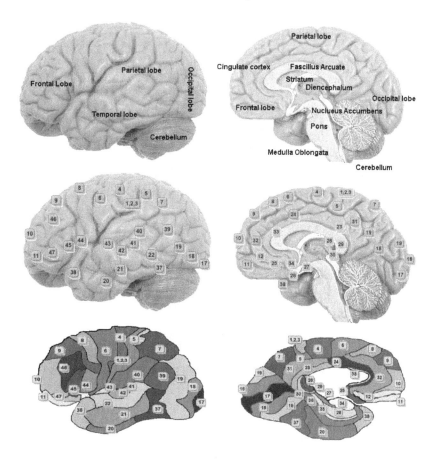

Figure 3.3 The columnar organization of the cortex.

incoming and outgoing connections to other cortical columns or subcortical neurons. In addition, the physiology of the cells composing
a column is also dependent on the type of transmitter used to propagate information from the presynaptic terminals to the dendrites.
For example, dopamine is used to transmit information in circuits
involved in reward estimation. Columnar activity is also influenced
by the different kinds of neuromodulator than modifying neuronal
activity. For example, catecholamine may control ionic movements
at the synaptic level in order to modulate the intensity of the local
ionic currents. Further information about the physiology of cortical
columns may be found in Rocha *et al.* (1998, 2004).

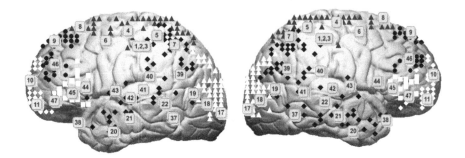

Figure 3.4   Deciding how to satisfy needs.

Due to the diversity of columnar specialization, it is now well established that the cortex functions as a distributed processing device, with the different types of columns specializing in distinct kinds of information processing and the complexity of the calculations being carried out by the brain depending not only on the type of column enrolled to contribute to cortical processing, but mostly how they are organized in time and space for such a purpose (Rocha *et al.*, 1998, 2004).

Cortical columns located at different cortical areas specialize in processing distinct types of information. See text for further details.

It has been established that neurons located at BA 11 (white diamonds in Figure 3.4) encode preferences or values of services or goods concerning their set G of goals. In addition, it has been reported that neurons located at BA 10 (white diamonds in Figure 3.4) are in charge of handling expected rewards or benefits associated to goods and services concerning the necessities created by the environment H considering G. Finally, neurons located at BA 13 (Insula) and Amigdala enroll for calculating the risk associated to these goods or services. In this context, neurons located at BA 11 enroll for determining motivation to act in order to satisfy the need or necessity to obtain the goods or services required by G, while cells at BA 10, BA 13 and Amigdala take charge of computing benefits provided by these services and goods and risks associated with them.

Columns of BA 9 and BA 36 (black circles in Figure 3.4) have being described like related with activities required by working memory that is in charge of handling key information supporting reasoning. In this context, neurons at these cortical areas may be assumed to use information provided by BA 10, 11 and Amigdala to calculated adequacy of acting to obtained required goods and services and to coordinate the recruitment of neurons from other cortical and subcortical areas to implement planned reasoning.

Columns at BA 8 (black triangles in Figure 3.4) are related with reasoning under uncertainty. BA 8 uses information provided by those neurons estimating benefit and risk to calculate the amount of uncertainty in decision-making. Uncertainty calculated by BA 8 controls activity of neurons located at BA 6 (black triangles in Figure 3.4) that are in charge of attention control. These neurons may be assumed to modulate the activities of columns located at BA 5 and 7 (black triangles in Figure 3.4) that act as hubs to access information from semantic and episodic memories.

Neurons at BA 39, 40, 41, 42 and 43 (black diamonds in Figure 3.4) are reported to be involved in arithmetic calculations required by task solving as well as by computation of probabilities of observable events. These neurons may be recruited by neurons in working memory circuits to support calculations required by decision-making. This way, neurons located at BA 20, 21, 22 and 37 are related with the linguistic encoding of such calculations (black diamonds in Figure 3.4).

Rocha *et al.* (1998, 2004) also argue that the neural encoding of any kind of useful information (sensory, temporal or spatial) about the environment H may be formalized by means a formal grammar $F(G)$. In this context, knowledge about how to act or how to understand incoming information is encoded as sentences $s(F(G))$ accepted by such grammar $F(G)$. Cortical columns located at BA 44 and 45 (white squares in Figure 3.4) are involved in syntactic and semantic analyses of such sentences (Rocha *et al.*, 2004, 2011). Neurons located at these areas may also recruit cells from BA 20, 21, 22, 37, 39 and 40 (language and vision $\rightarrow$ face recognition) to support $s(F(G))$ analysis.

Finally, columns located at BA 17, 18 and 19 (white triangles in Figure 3.4) are related with visual analysis of all information required to support all computations described above, and BA 47 (white squares in Figure 3.4) is involved with selecting the best solution to satisfy the necessities created by the environment H considering G.

3.5   The Properties of Distributed Intelligent Processing Systems

The theory of Distributed Intelligent Processing Systems (DIPS) was first developed in the field of artificial intelligence to formalize those systems comprised by multiple agents that individually have some sort of expertize in solving defined problems, but if working together they may solve tasks of higher complexity (Rocha *et al.*, 2004). DIPS intelligence is a function of the types of tools used by its agents as well as of how and for what purpose these tools are used (Rocha *et al.*, 2011). Financial decision is a task supported by DIPS (Figure 3.5), because neurons in different parts of the brain specialize in the specific tasks required for such a purpose, and how each decision is made depends on how they enroll in the reasoning depending on the actual environmental conditions and previous experiences.

Central to the concept of a DIPS is the proposal that reasoning is supported by the cooperative activity of a collection of agents, each having a specific knowledge or tool useful in handling a complex

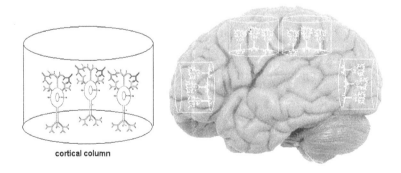

cortical column

Figure 3.5   The brain as a distributed intelligent processing system (DIPS).

task that is of interest of the whole system (Rocha *et al.*, 2004). Processing is decentralized and cooperation is dynamic. Agents enroll or are recruited to support reasoning if their knowledge or ability may contribute to handle the task in question. The same agents may contribute to the solution of different tasks but different types of reasoning have also to recruit distinct types of agents.

As discussed in the previous section, neurons located at different areas of the brain specialize in handling specific tasks associated with decision-making. According to the model in Figure 3.5, neurons belonging to sensory systems continuously scan the environment H collecting a large set of sensory data that are matched to information stored by neurons in the self-memory circuits specifying the individual goals (G). Neurons located at BA 7 and 19, in the area identified as Precuneus, act as hubs for accessing memory data distributed on many sensory and associative cortical areas. Necessities of goods and services to maintain these goals are then identified and triggers reasoning about alternative actions that may contribute to satisfy these necessities, using knowledge acquired from previous experiences.

Neurons at BA 11 take charge of computing value and preferences for services and goods, taking into consideration the goals in G and because of this, they will be requested to enroll in any reasoning about how to fulfill needs created by H concerning G.

Neurons at BA 10, 13 and Amigdala are associated to computing benefit and risk of actions considered as possible solution for this kind of reasoning. Neurons at BA 39, 40, 41, 42 and 43 may be recruited to carry out the computations required to calculate value, risk and benefit of each of the actions assumed to possibly fulfill actual needs. Neurons located at BA 9, 44, 45 and 46 encode information about how to coordinate reasoning about acting and cells at BA 47 enroll for selecting the best course of action to fulfill actual needs. The implementation of this course of action generates a new string of sensory data that is used to monitor DIPS behavior and the success (or not) of the decision-making, by comparing expected and experienced benefits and risk, recruiting again neurons in BA 10, 11, 13 and Amigdala. If benefits are higher than risk, then connections between neurons enrolled in decision-making are strengthened, thereby increasing the probability of the same course of action to be implemented to try to satisfy the same or similar needs, but if the risks are superior to the benefits, then the connections between enrolled neurons are reduced.

There is no DIPS central storage of knowledge or data. Part of DIPS knowledge relies on agent specialization and part of them is encoded by relations shared by their agents. Relationship among agents has to be easily modified whenever necessary to support learning. Any DIPS control is logically and geographically distributed. Control is not a property of specific agents, but it is embedded in the rule for message passing among agents. Messages are exchanged directly because agents are directly connected (mailing address systems) or by means of blackboard agents (working memory systems). Agents may enroll on reasoning attending messages posted on blackboards, e.g., working memory, are recruited by agents that know about their abilities. Message exchange results in oscillatory activity between sets of agents.

DIPS knowledge is encoded both by the tools agents have to solve tasks as well as by how these neurons may connect to each other. This means that knowledge is stored by specialized neurons in distinct areas of the brain and by modulating synaptic strength between them. Successful neuronal association results in increasing the amount of chemicals (transmitters) at presynaptic terminals that facilitate neuronal connection. Unsuccessful cooperation between neurons results in decreasing the amount of such chemicals. These changes are promoted by neuromodulators that may modify gene reading (Figure 3.6). Some neural circuits may act as blackboards for knowledge sharing as neurons at BA 9 and 46 compose the working memory systems and cells at Precuneus act hubs for memory access.

3.6   Neural Networks

Neurons at different cortical areas and subcortical structures are heavily interconnected in a huge network that supports brain as a DIPS. These interconnections are provided by an intensive axon

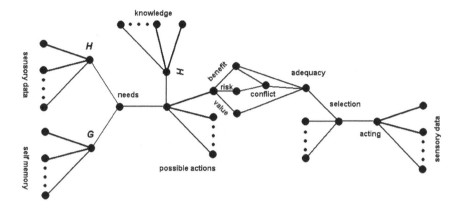

Figure 3.6 Electrical properties of the neuron.

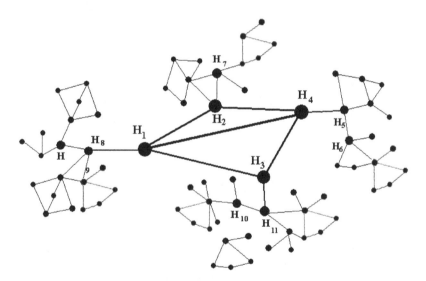

Figure 3.7 Scale-free network has some heavily connected nodes called hubs (*H*) to improve message exchange among agents (nodes).

branching that connects each set of neurons to a large number of other neurons located in both near and distant locations.

To reduce the costs of this massive neuronal interconnection, nature developed some kind of networks that are very efficient in spreading information among their nodes using some preferential interconnection between some special nodes that function as hubs for message spread (Figure 3.7). Hubs may be classified according to the size of their connections with other agents. Efficient networks have low number of highly connected hubs. Connectivity of the other hubs decreases rapidly in a nonlinear manner. This reduces costs of developing and maintaining connection pathways.

Scale-free and broad-range networks are examples of nets that are very efficient in message spreading at a low connectivity cost because connectivity of their hubs decreases in a power law manner (Albert and Barbárasi, 1999; Iturria *et al.*, 2008). Rocha *et al.* (2010) showed that calculated $h(e_i)$ distribution has a power law pattern that characterizes scale-free and/or broad-range networks.

References

Albert, R., Barabási, A. (1999). Statistical mechanics of complex networks. *Reviews of Modern Physics* 74(1), 47–97.

Iturria-Medina, Y., Sotero, R. C., Canales-Rodriguez, E. J., Aleman-Gomez, Y. R., Melie-Garca, L. (2008). Studying the human brain anatomical network viadiffusion-weighted MRI and Graph Theory. *NeuroImage* 40, 1064–1076.

Rocha, A. (1992). *Neural Nets: A Theory for Brains and Machine. Lecture Notes in Artificial Intelligence.* vol. 638, Springer-Verlag, Berlin, Heidelberg, Germany.

Rocha, A., Rebelo, M., Miura, K. (1998). Toward a theory of molecular computing. *Information Sciences*, 106, 123–157.

Rocha, A., Pereira Jr., A., Coutinho, F. (2001). NMDA channel and consciousness: From signal coincidence detection to quantum computing. *Progress in Neurobiology*, 64, 555–573.

Rocha, A., Massad, E., Pereira, Jr., A. (2004). *The Brain: From Fuzzy Arithmetic to Quantum Computing.* Springer-Verlag, Heidelberg, Germany.

Rocha, A., Rocha, F., Massad, E., Burattini, M. (2010). Neurodynamics of an election. *Brain Research*, 1351, 198–211.

Rocha, A., Rocha, F., Massad, E. (2011). The brain as a distributed intelligent processing system: An EEG study. *PLoS ONE*, 6(3), e17355.

Chapter 4

The Brain as a Distributed Processing System

Neuroscience is a branch of science that has its origins in the work of Paul Broca (Price, 2012) reporting that lesion of the left inferior frontal area (Brodmann areas 44 and 45 in Figure 4.1) impaired speech in his patient nicknamed Ton-Ton, because this was the only sound he was able to produce. This initial observation was followed by the report made by Carl Wernicke that lesion of the left temporal lobe (Brodmann area 22 near areas 39 and 40 in Figure 4.1) impaired human capacity to understand spoken languages. These initial observations provided background for a reductionist view of brain function that tries to assign complex cognitive functions to specific and unique areas of the brain.

In contrast to this theoretical approach, Gestalt theory (Humphrey, 1924) proposed that mind forms a global whole of self-organizing tendencies, and no specific complex cognitive function can be assigned to specific brain areas.

As discussed in Chapter 3, the theory of distributed intelligent processing system (DIPS) was first developed in the field of artificial intelligence to formalize those systems comprised by multiple agents that individually have some sort of expertize in solving defined problems, and working together they may solve tasks of higher complexity (Rocha *et al.*, 2004). In this theoretical approach, complex cognitive functions are tasks to be handled by widely distributed set of neurons that are in charge of handling specific subsets of problems. This is the theoretical approach used in this book.

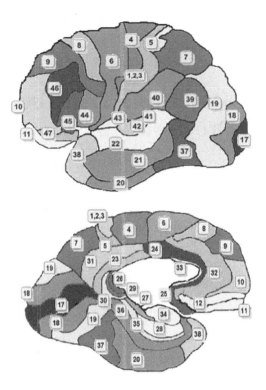

Figure 4.1　Brodmann areas.

4.1　Segmenting Cortex into Brodmann Areas

Brodmann (1909) has shown the huge structural diversity of the cortex classifying 52 different cellular arrangements having distinct cortical localizations (Figure 4.1). Some of them are large (BA 21), whereas some others are small (BA 26). Different Brodmann areas participate together in specific neural circuits in charge of handling specific cognitive subtasks. Let us discuss some of these circuits and subtasks.

4.2　Value, Benefit and Risk Assessment

Value, benefit and risk are important variables influencing financial decision-making, and neuroscience has shown that they are processed at distinct locations (Figure 4.2) at BA 10 and 11 that are, in general,

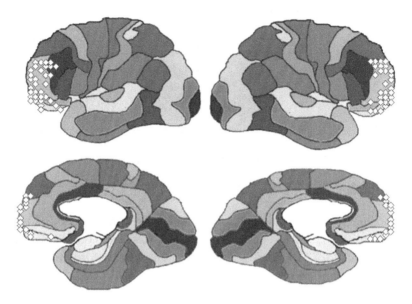

Figure 4.2 Location of cortical neurons involved in value, benefit and risk assessment.

called ventromedial prefrontal cortex (vmPFC) (Abitbol *et al.*, 2015; Howard *et al.*, 2015; Monosov and Hikosaka, 2012; Phelps *et al.*, 2004; Sokol-Hessner *et al.*, 2012; Winecoff *et al.*, 2013).

Neurons at ventral part of vmPFC, especially BA 10, are assumed to process expected or experienced rewards, whereas their dorsal part seems to be involved in sensing expected or experienced risk assessment. Furthermore, within ventral vmPFC, posterior neurons encode probability of reward, whereas anterior neurons encoded possibility of risk. Neurons in BA 11 are involved in assigning values to goods and services upon which preferences are calculated.

vmPFC contribute differentially to the processing of emotional valence (Monosov and Hikosaka, 2012). Because of this, its neurons are also reported to be involved in determining right and wrong (Lim *et al.*, 2013; Rocha *et al.*, 2013a) and true and false (Koscik and Tranel, 2012; Ribas *et al.*, 2013; Rocha *et al.*, 2014).

Some neurons located at the dorsolateral BA 10 are proposed to participate on the circuits of working memory (WM). While BA 10 and 11 are involved in evaluating risk aversion, Insula (Figure 4.3)

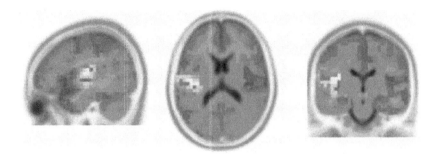

Figure 4.3   Insula is activated in the case of expected or experienced losses.

is reported to be a key structure in loss-aversion calculation (Paulus and Stein, 2006). Here, it is assumed that risk aversion is related to the possibility of falling in reaching a goal, whereas loss aversion is related to the possibility of harm and losses.

4.3   Working Memory

WM (Figure 4.4) is the system that is responsible for the transient holding and processing of information concerning a cognitive task (Baddeley, 1992) and it involves neurons located at BA 9, 10 and 46 (D'Esposito *et al.*, 1998; Jonides *et al.*, 1993; Ranganath *et al.*, 2003).

WM neurons have connections with other cells distributed over the entire brain that are specifically involved in processing sensory and motor information. In this line of reasoning, neurons at WM have the address (connections) to retrieve information stored in long-term memory and semantic memory. They may enroll neurons involved with calculations and spatial and temporal location of data, stored in many distinct cortical areas. Because of this, WM is assumed to be part of the executive system (Baddeley, 1996) defined as a circuit in charge of controlling execution of any cognitive task.

4.4   Attention Control

Uncertainty is the most influential variable on attention control because it signals necessity to scan for information that reduces

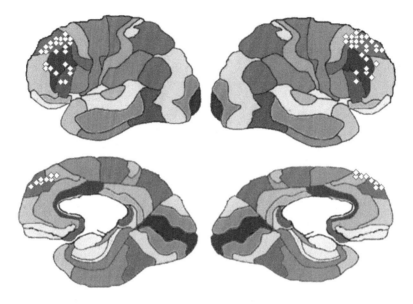

Figure 4.4 WM system.

conflict determining reasoning. The amount of conflict is proportional to the ratio of activity between the vmPFC circuits involved in determining emotional valence (good or bad, right or wrong) of the information being processed. Conflicts increase as this ratio approaches 1 (Rocha *et al.*, 2009).

Attention control neural circuit involves neurons distributed over the anterior cingulate cortex (ACC), BA 8 and 6 (Figure 4.5) and it is another component of the executive system (Aarts *et al.*, 2009; Hopfinger *et al.*, 2000; Milham *et al.*, 2001; Wang *et al.*, 2009).

According to Rocha *et al.* (2009) and Rocha (2013), ACC is in charge of computing conflict, while BA 8 uses this information to rank uncertainties in order to control activity of neurons at BA 6. These later neurons are responsible to enroll sensory and memory systems in searching for information to change emotional valences and to reduce conflicts. Motor actions are triggered in the case of searching for new sensory information, especially eye movements (Thompson *et al.*, 2005) because vision is a very important source of data to humans.

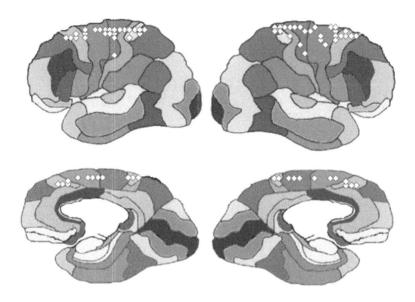

Figure 4.5 Attention control.

4.5 Memory Access

Knowledge and memory in a DIPS are distributed among its agents (or neurons in the case of brain). Neurons from each sensory, motor, associative and evaluation system that enroll in the solution of a (un)success task have their connection (un)strengthened to encode knowledge or store a memory. This way, it may be assumed that innumerous specific circuits of widespread neurons encode specific pieces of knowledge or memories (Cavanna and Trimble, 2006; Fletcher *et al.*, 1997; Moscovitch *et al.*, 2005). Some of the neurons may become specialized in controlling access to encode and rehearsal these specific pieces of information, like BA 7 and 19 (also named Precuneus) because they act as hubs in these networks (Svoboda *et al.*, 2006; Utevsky *et al.*, 2014) and because they are involved in attention control, like BA 6 and 8 (Figure 4.6).

4.6 Arithmetic Calculation

Arithmetic calculation is a process that depends on a distributed number representation in the brain (Rocha and Massad, 2003; Rocha

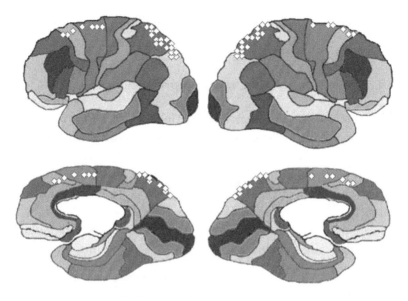

Figure 4.6 Memory access.

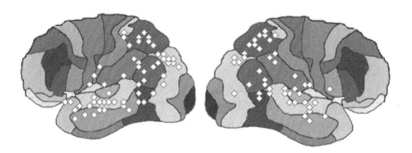

Figure 4.7 Cortical areas involved in arithmetic calculation.

et al., 2004, 2005) involving areas located mostly at the temporal and parietal cortices (Figure 4.7). Rocha *et al.* (2005) proposed that neurons at these locations, essentially BA 7, 21, 22, 37, 39, 40, 41, 42 and 43, participate in different neural circuits under control of BA 6 (attention control), BA 46 (WM) and BA 47 (inhibitory control) that are in charge of quantity representation and the different arithmetic calculations (Baldo and Dronkers, 2007; Hanakawa *et al.*, 2002).

They are also involved in computing linear functions (Rocha *et al.*, 2005).

4.7   Language Production and Comprehension

Recent studies using functional magnetic resonance imaging (fMRI), magnetoencephalography and electroencephalography (EEG) have expanded our knowledge about the neural circuits enrolled in language comprehension and production by demonstrating that these cognitive activities involve a large number of areas, in addition to Broca's (BA 44 and 45) and Wernick's (BA 22) areas (Price, 2012). The large number of different types of neurons involved in language, understanding and production, as well as the complex dynamics of their relations points to the distributed character of language processing (Figure 4.8). Most of the time, humans use language and visual information complementarily. This is because language production and comprehension enrolls neurons at both hemispheres despite the fact that linguistic processing is mostly a task for the left hemisphere (Foz *et al.*, 2002; Price, 2012).

4.8   Acting

Mirror neurons were originally described as neurons that fire both when an action is performed and when a similar or identical action is passively observed. They are neither sensory nor motor neurons,

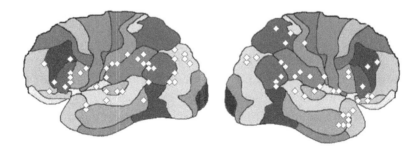

Figure 4.8   Semantic processing: verbal (left) and visual (right).

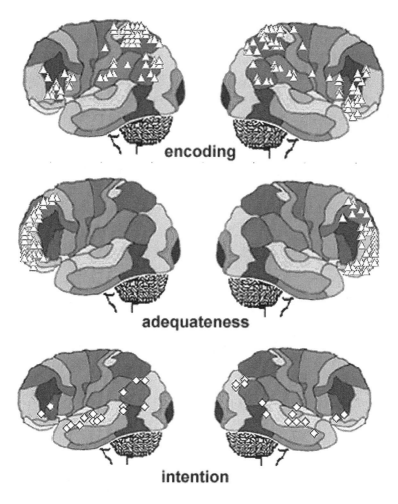

Figure 4.9 Action handling system.

but associative neurons linking perception (of sensory information) to action (motor output). Because of this, they are part of a network of brain regions (Figure 4.9), called here action handling system, that possess properties associated with action observation and execution (Figure 4.9). Additional areas are recruited to assess action adequateness to actual environment or reasoning upon which intention to act is calculated.

Mirror neurons are mostly located at the parietal lobule (mostly BA 39 and 40), temporal cortex (BA 22), inferior frontal gyrus (mostly at BA 44 and 45) and the adjacent ventral premotor cortex (BA 6). These neurons are considered in charge of encoding components of actions involving both sensorial and motor information.

Neurons located at BA 10 are proposed, here, to encode benefit and risk associated with acting (Rocha *et al.*, 2009, 2013a), whereas neurons at BA 11 are supposed to value action according to motivation triggered by a necessity to reach or maintain a goal (Rocha *et al.*, 2009, 2013a,b). Based on these pieces of information, neurons at ACC calculate conflicts (Rocha *et al.*, 2009, 2014).

Information about value, benefit, risk and conflicts is used by neurons located at BA 8 to calculate uncertainty about action that is used by BA 6 to control attention and memory access and by neurons at BA 9 to calculate adequateness of acting.

Using information provided by all subcircuits described above, neurons distributed mostly over BA 39, 40, 44 and 45 take charge of calculating intention to act.

4.9   Assessing Other Actions

Theory of mind (ToM) has its origins in the paper published by Premack and Woodruff (1978) to refer to the ability of attributing mental states to oneself and others and to understand that others may have beliefs, desires, intentions and perspectives that are different from one's own.

Although ToM has been criticized on both conceptual and experimental terms, EEG and fMRI studies revealed that neurons located at vmPFC (BA 10 and 11), inferior frontal cortex (BA 47), at basal temporal pole (BA 38) and at the junction of temporal and parietal lobules (BA 39 and 40) are engaged in complex computations about self and other's intention to act (Figure 4.10). There is a considerable overlap of cortical areas involved in processing actions as discussed in the previous session and those reported as supporting ToM (for this purpose, compare Figures 4.9 and 4.10).

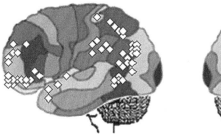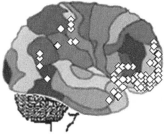

Figure 4.10   Neurons involved in social cognition.

Assuming that we mostly know about ourselves throughout the inner talk that we constantly maintain, the motor actions we execute and information obtained by sensing our body, it is reasonable to assume that most of self-cognition is mostly dependent on left hemisphere activity. In contrast, we obtain information about others' behavior mostly by visual and auditory systems. Because of this, it is reasonable to assume that social cognition is mostly dependent on right hemisphere activity. This may explain why cortical activity is a little bit different when left and right hemispheres are compared in Figure 4.10, showing the cortical areas involved in dilemma judgment (Rocha *et al.*, 2013a).

4.10   Reasoning as a Cooperative Action between Specialized Circuits

We have discussed in the previous sections how neural subsystems specialized in processing some basic common reasoning subtasks are organized in the brain. Financial reasoning is a very complex task that requires assessment of expected or experienced values, benefits, risks and losses of services and goods required to satisfy our needs. Besides, we have to select best options and avoid bad ones. Once choice is made, it is necessary to implement and monitor the course of action. All of this demands large amount of calculations and sometimes the use of oral and/or written language. Because of that, financial reasoning is a cognitive task recruiting neurons (Figure 4.11) distributed all over the brain (Rocha *et al.*, 2013b).

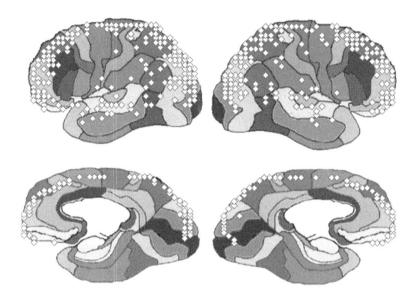

Figure 4.11   Financial reasoning.

Some of the subsystems are active during most of the reasoning such as the Evaluation subsystem involving BA 10 and 11, since it is recruited for assessment of values, benefits and risks as well as deciding about true/false or right/wrong statements. Some other subsystems will be active only during specific reasoning phases, e.g., those requiring calculations.

References

Aarts, E., Roelofs, A., Van Turennout, M. (2009). Attentional control of task and response in lateral and medial frontal cortex: Brain activity and reaction time distributions. *Neuropsychologia*, 47, 2089–2099.

Abitbol R., Lebreton, M., Hollard, G., Richmond, B., Bouret, S., Pessiglione, M. (2015). Neural mechanisms underlying contextual dependency of subjective values: Converging evidence from monkeys and humans. *Journal of Neuroscience*, 35, 2308–2320.

Baddeley A. (1992). Working memory. *Science*, 255, 556–559.

Baddeley. A. (1996). Exploring the central executive. *The Quarterly Journal of Experimental Psychology*, 49, 5–28.

Baldo, J., Dronkers, N. (2007). Neural correlates of arithmetic and language comprehension: A common substrate? *Neuropsychologia*, 45, 229–235.

Brodmann K. (1909). *Vergleichende Lokalisationslehre der Grosshirnrinde.* Johann Ambrosius Bart, Leipzig.

Cavanna, A., Trimble, M. (2006). The precuneus: A review of its functional anatomy and behavioural correlates. *Brain*, 129, 564–583.

D'Esposito, M., Aguirre, G., Zarahn, E., Ballard, D., Shin, R., Lease, J. (1998). Functional MRI studies of spatial and nonspatial working memory. *Cognitive Brain Research*, 7, 1–13.

Fletcher, P., Frith, C., Rugg, M. (1997). The functional neuroanatomy of episodic memory tins. *Functional Anatomy of Memory*, 20, 1213–1217.

Foz, F., Lucchini, B., Palimieri, S., Rocha, A., Rodella, E., Rondó, A., Cardoso, M., Ramazzini, P., Leite, C. (2002). Language plasticity revealed by EEG mapping. *Pediatric Neurology*, 26, 106–115.

Hanakawa, T., Honda, M., Sawamoto, N., Okada, T., Yonekura, Y., Fukuyama, H., Shibasaki, H. (2002). The role of rostral Brodmann area 6 in mental-operation tasks: An integrative neuroimaging approach. *Cerebral Cortex*, 12, 1157–1170.

Hopfinger, J., Buonocore, M., Mangun, G. (2000). The neural mechanisms of top-down attentional control. *Nature Neuroscience*, 3, 284–294.

Howard, J., Gottfried, J., Tobler, P., Kahnt, T. (2015). Identity-specific coding of future rewards in the human orbitofrontal cortex. *PNAS*, 112, 5195–5200.

Humphrey, G. (1924). The psychology of the gestalt. *Journal of Educational Psychology*, 15(7), 401–412.

Jonides, J., Smith, E., Koeppe, R., Awh, E., Minoshima, S., Mintun, M. (1993). Spatial working-memory in humans as revealed by PE. *Nature*, 363(6430), 623–625.

Koscik, T., Tranel, D. (2012). The human ventromedial prefrontal cortex is critical for transitive inference. *Journal Cognitive Neuroscience*, 24, 1191–1204.

Lim, S., O'Doherty, J., Rangel, A. (2013). Stimulus value signals in ventromedial PFC reflect the integration of attribute value signals computed in fusiform gyrus and posterior superior temporal gyrus. *The Journal of Neuroscience*, 33, 8729–8741.

Milham, M., Banich, M., Webb, A., Barad, V., Cohen, N., Wszalek, T., Kramer, A. (2001). The relative involvement of anterior cingulate and prefrontal cortex in attentional control depends on nature of conflict. *Cognitive Brain Research*, 12, 467–473.

Monosov, I., Hikosaka, O. (2012). Regionally distinct processing of rewards and punishments by the primate ventromedial prefrontal cortex. *Journal of Neuroscience*, 30, 10318–10330.

Moscovitch, M., Rosenbaum, S., Gilboa, A., Addis, D., Westmacott, R., Grady, C., Mcandrews, M., Levine, B., Black, S., Winocur, G., Nadel, N. (2005). Functional neuroanatomy of remote episodic, semantic and spatial memory: A unified account based on multiple trace theory. *Journal of Anatomy*, 207, 35–66.

Paulus, M., Stein, M. (2006). An insular view of anxiety. *Biological Psychiatry*, 60(4), 383–387.

Phelps, E., Delgado, M., Nearing, K., Ledoux, J. (2004). Extinction learning in humans: Role of the amygdala and vmPFC. *Neuron*, 43, 897–905.

Price, C. (2012). A review and synthesis of the first 20 years of pet and fMRI studies of heard speech, spoken language and reading. *Neuroimage*, 62, 816–847.

Premack, D., Woodruff, G. (1978). Does the chimpanzee have a theory of mind? *Behavioral and Brain Sciences*, 1(4), 515–526.

Ranganath, C., Johnson, M., D'Esposito, M. (2003). Prefrontal activity associated with working memory and episodic long-term memory. *Neuropsychologia*, 41, 378–389.

Ribas, L., Rocha, F., Ortega, N., Rocha, A., Massad, E. (2013). Brain activity and medical diagnosis: An EEG study. *BMC Neuroscience*, 14, 109.

Rocha, A., Massad, E. (2003). How the human brain is endowed for mathematical reasoning. *Mathematics Today*, 39, 81–84.

Rocha, A., Massad, E., Pereira Jr., A. (2004). *The Brain: From Fuzzy Arithmetic to Quantum Computing*. Springer, Heidelberg, Germany.

Rocha, F., Rocha, A., Massad, E., Menezes, R. (2005). Brain mappings of the arithmetic processing in children and adults. *Cognitive Brain Research*, 22, 359–372.

Rocha, A., Burattini, M., Rocha, F., Massad, E. (2009). A neuroeconomic modeling of attention deficit and hyperactivity disorder. *Journal of Biological Systems*, 17, 597–621.

Rocha, A. (2013). What we learn about global systemic risk with neurosciences. Neuroeconomics. *Ejournal Financial Crises Ejournal*, 2(90). http://Papers. Ssrn.Com/Abstract=2316765.

Rocha, A., Rocha, F., Massad, E. (2013a). Moral dilemma judgment revisited: A Loret ta analysis. *Journal of Behavioral and Brain Science*, 3(8), 624–640.

Rocha, A., Vieito, J., Rocha, F. (2013b). Brain activity follow up of stock market financial variables. http://ssrn.com/abstract=2329873.

Rocha, A., Massad, E., Rocha, F., Burattini, M. (2014). Brain and law: An EEG study of how we decide or not to implement a law. *Journal Behavioral and Brain Science*, 4, 559–578.

Sokol-Hessner, P., Hutcherson, C., Hare, T., Rangel, A. (2012). Decision value computation in dlPFC and vmPFC adjusts to the available decision time. *European Journal of Neuroscience*, 35, 1065–1074.

Svoboda, E., Mckinnon, M., Levine, B. (2006). The functional neuroanatomy of autobiographical memory: A meta-analysis. *Neuropsychologia*, 44, 2189–2208.

Thompson, K., Biscoe, K., Sato, T. (2005). Neuronal basis of covert spatial attention in the frontal eye field. *Journal of Neuroscience*, 25, 9479–9487.

Utevsky, A., Smith, D., Huettel, S. (2014). Precuneus is a functional core of the default-mode network. *Journal of Neuroscience*, 34(3), 932–940.

Wang, L., Liu, X., Guisel, K., Knight, T., Ghajar, J., Fan, J. (2009). Effective connectivity of the fronto-parietal network during attentional control. *Journal of Cognitive Neuroscience*, 22(3), 543–553.

Winecoff, A., Clithero, J., Carter, R., Bergman, S., Wang, L., Huettel, S. (2013). Ventromedial prefrontal cortex encodes emotional value. *Journal of Neuroscience*, 27, 11032–11039.

Chapter 5

How to Map the Brain

The purpose of this chapter is to discuss techniques that are being used to scan brain activity associated with financial decision-making, such as positron emission tomography (PET), single-photon emission computed tomography (SPECT), functional magnetic resonance imaging (fMRI) and electroencephalography (EEG).

5.1 Positron Emission Tomography and Single-Photon Emission Computed Tomography

PET is a technique that produces a 3D image of functional processes in the body by detecting gamma rays emitted indirectly by a positron-emitting molecule (tracer) that is injected into the blood stream. The most commonly used radiotracer in PET scanning is fluorodeoxyglucose, an analogue of glucose. The concentrations of tracer will indicate tissue metabolic activity by virtue of the regional glucose uptake. Limitations to the widespread use of PET arise from the high costs of cyclotrons needed to produce tracers and their short live. In addition, PET has to be obtained in combination with computed tomography (CT) scan that furnishes the image of the structure of the activated area.

SPECT measures gamma activity emitted by radioisotope, in general, attached to a specific ligand. SPECT imaging is performed by using a gamma camera to acquire multiple 2D images in multiple angles and a reconstruction computation is used to create a 3D image from the multiple data sets. The technique requires delivery of the radioisotope into the patient, normally through injection into the bloodstream.

The main differences between these two techniques is that in SPECT every single arising photon is counted, whereas PET imaging uses pairs of photons and only pairs will be detected as a valid signal. However, both techniques are not frequently used to study decision-making, because they require injection of a radioactive drugs into the blood stream.

5.2 Using Functional Magnet Resonance Image

fMRI measures changes in blood flow associated to brain activity to infer about the areas involved in a specific reasoning (Figure 5.1). The most used technique for such a purpose records change between

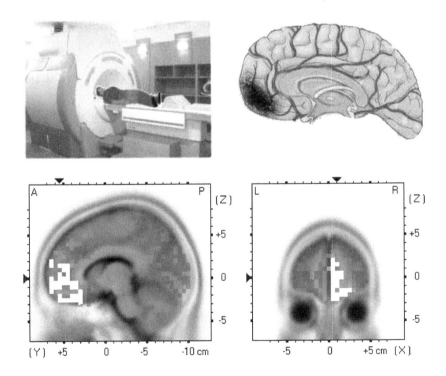

Figure 5.1   fMRI technique.

oxygen-rich and oxygen-poor blood and it is usually called BOLD technique. The resulting difference is color coding and it is assumed to measure the strength of activation across the brain or the specific studied region. The technique may localize activity within millimeters but, using standard techniques, it takes at least a time window of 1–2 s, since it takes that long for the vascular system to respond to the brain's need for glucose. This response typically rises to a peak at about 5 s after the stimulus. If the neurons keep firing, from a continuous stimulus, for instance, the peak spreads to a flat plateau while the neurons stay active. After activity stops, the BOLD signal falls below the original level, the baseline, a phenomenon called undershoot.

fMRI spatial resolution is determined by the size of voxels which is a 3D rectangular cuboid, whose dimensions are set by the slice thickness, the area of a slice and the grid imposed on the slice by the scanning process. A voxel typically contains a few million neurons.

The temporal resolution is the smallest time period of neural activity reliably separated out by fMRI, and for any technique used to process the data, it is always above 1 s. Two main techniques are used in fMRI studies.

Block design: two or more conditions are alternated in blocks. Each block will have duration of a certain number of fMRI scans and within each block, only one condition is presented. By making the conditions differ only in the cognitive process of interest, the fMRI signal that differentiates the conditions should represent this cognitive process of interest.

Event-related design: two or more conditions are presented sequentially allowing more real-world testing, however the statistical power of event-related designs is inherently low, because BOLD changes following a single stimulus presentation is small.

Both block and event-related designs are based on the subtraction paradigm. This paradigm assumes that activity of different cognitive processes can be added, such that BOLD differences between experimental conditions reveal brain activity associated with the cognitive process that differentiates these conditions.

Company	Ind	Var	Value	S	B	
INDEX	0,96	-0,01				
BANIF	1,04	0,00	22,01	○	○	OK

s_3

Company	Ind	Var	Value	S	B	
INDEX	0,96	-0,01				
Energias de Portugal	1,00	-0,01	22,01	○	○	OK

s_6

Figure 5.2 Block design to study financial decision-making.

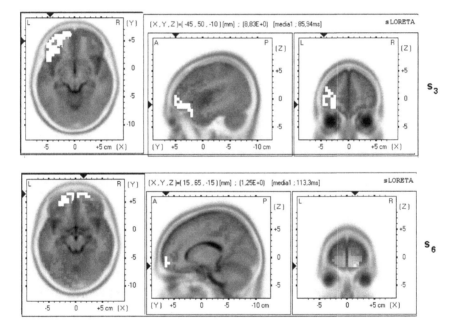

Figure 5.3 Results from an fMRI study on financial decision.

Let us consider an fMRI design to study brain activity associated with buying (pressing button B in Figure 5.2), selling (pressing button S) or holding (pressing button OK) stocks in $market_1$, $market_2$. Subtraction paradigm requires recording BOLD changes associated with buying, selling or holding one given stock each time (e.g., stocks s_2 and s_6 in Figure 5.3) and asking the volunteer to make a decision in a fixed time (greater than 1 s) after information is presented, independent of the difficulty he/she may have to choose the type of transaction.

Now, we may use block paradigm creating blocks where volatility of each stock varies between blocks if stocks of similar volatility are used in each block but mean volatility is different among blocks. For instance, we may compose one block with stocks s_3, s_4 and s_7 in market$_1$ and another block with stocks s_1 and s_5 in market$_1$ plus s_6 in market$_2$. In the same way, we may use event-related paradigm by sequentially interpolating stock s_3, s_4 and s_7 with stocks s_1, s_5 and s_6.

The rationality is that the two set of stocks will be associated to different BOLD responses in areas that are involved in handling volatility (e.g., responses associated with s_3 and s_6; Figure 5.3). In the experiment simulated in Figure 5.4, neurons at BA 11 would be assumed to be related with volatility because BOLD response for s_3 is greater than that for s_6. Seed choice is complex, what makes this kind of analysis unusual in neuroeconomics and makes multiple regression analysis, if not impossible, at least very difficult.

fMRI studies have shown that BA 10 is related with value assessment of services and good (Figure 5.4); neurons at Amygdale and Insula correlate both to expected or experienced risks; activation

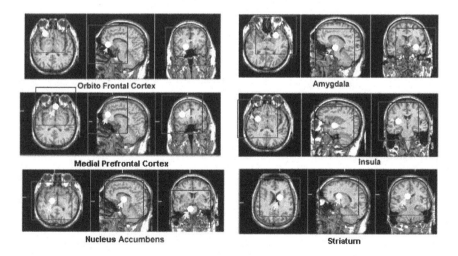

Figure 5.4 Some results from the literature on financial decision-making.

of neurons at Nucleus Accumbens correlates both to expected or experienced rewards, and striatal neurons are enrolled in trust evaluation (Breiter *et al.*, 2001; Burgess *et al.*, 2011; FitzGerald *et al.*, 2010; Knutson, 2007; Knutson and Bossaerts, 2007; Knutson *et al.*, 2003, 2005, 2007; Kuhnen and Knutson, 2005; Mcclure *et al.*, 2004; Polezzi *et al.*, 2010; Preuschoff *et al.*, 2006; Samanez-Larkin *et al.*, 2010; Seymour and McClure, 2008; Tobler *et al.*, 2007).

5.3   Using EEG

One of the first investigations that join neuroscience and finance was done by Gehring and Willoughby (2002) using EEG, and many other studies have used this technique too (Bland and Schaefer, 2011; Cohen *et al.*, 2007, 2008; Davis *et al.*, 2011).

Neurons at the cortical columns are disposed perpendicular to the cortical surface and because of that the local ionic currents i_i of the neurons of each column are summed up. If the activity of a large number of adjacent columns in a certain cortical area is synchronously activated, then a huge number n of local ionic currents i_i are summed up in a large resulting current $i_r = \sum_{i=1}^{n} i_i$ that may propagate to the skull creating an electrical field $v_j(t) = w_j{}^*i_r$ under each electrode e_j positioned outside the skull that may be amplified and recorded (Figure 5.5). The value of $v_j(t)$ depends on the value of the electrical resistance between the electrode and the site of the activated columns. If columns at different cortical areas are simultaneously activated, then $v_j(t)$ becomes dependent on the activity at all these distinct areas, the contribution of each of them depending on the distance between the area and the electrode (Figure 5.5).

Let us consider an EEG design to study brain activity associated to financial decision for trading the stock market of a giver bourse (Figure 5.6). For such a purpose, volunteers receive an initial portfolio of 200 shares of seven different companies to play the game by making 50 trading decisions taking into consideration data presented in each 50 game screens in each experimental session (Figure 5.6). By holding, selling or buying stocks, volunteers may manipulate both

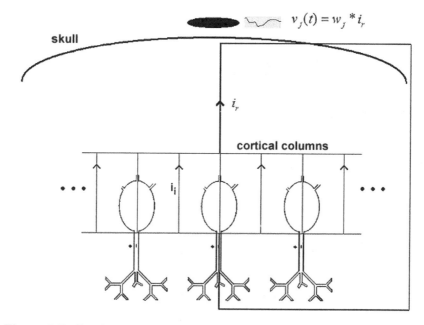

$$v_j(t) = w_j * i_r$$

skull

i_r

cortical columns

i_i

Figure 5.5 Local currents i_i generates the electrical field $v_j(t)$ recorded by the electrode over the skin.

Company	Ind	Var	Value	Qt	TOTAL	T-Qt	Price	S	B
INDEX	0,96	-0,01							
BANIF	1,04	0,00	22,01	200	4.402,39		EU	c	c
Portugal Telecom	1,63	0,04	34,93	200	6.985,11		EU	c	c
Energias de Portugal	0,94	-0,00	20,90	200	4.180,35		EU	c	c
Banco Comercial Português	1,11	0,00	7,28	200	1.455,84		EU	c	c
BRISA	1,01	-0,01	31,70	200	6.340,69		EU	c	c
Cimentos de Portugal	1,00	-0,01	8,35	200	1.670,99		EU	c	c
Futebol Clube do Porto	0,98	0,03	35,85	200	7.170,95		EU	c	c
				Fb	32.206,31		OK		
A				Pv	31.670,00				
18.330,00				C	536,31				

Figure 5.6 The screen of a stock market simulating game.

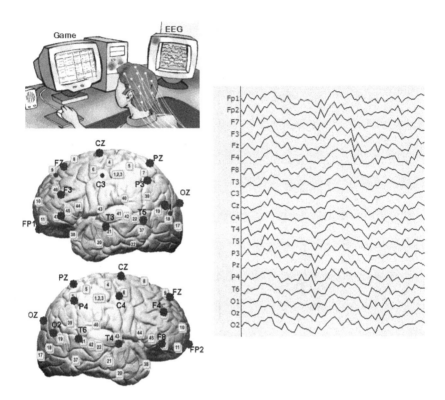

Figure 5.7 Recording the EEG with 20 electrodes while volunteer plays the stock market simulation game.

their *portfolio value* and *cash* in the attempt to have a *final balance =* *portfolio value* + *cash* greater than *market value*. This may be accomplished by both increasing *portfolio value* and/or *cash*. To make their decisions, volunteers select a company, set a price and the number of stocks to trade and press the button B to buy it or S to sell it, or just press the OK button to hold his portfolio.

Figure 5.7 exemplifies a simulation using EEG technology. In one part, we can see two computers, one to perform the simulation and the other to capture brain electrical activity with EEG. The graphic of the right size exemplifies what is possible to see in the computer that captures brain electrical frequencies. In this case, the image displays information about an EGG technology with 20 electrodes (Fp1, Fp2, etc.).

5.3.1 Event-related activity

Their EEG is recorded continuously during the entire experiment (Figure 5.7). According to Rocha *et al.* (2013), the best strategy to analyze it is to select information from 2 s of the recorded EEG prior to decision-making.

One of the techniques to analyze the EEG data is called event-related activity (ERA) and it consists in averaging the recorded EEG $v_j(t)$ epochs for each electrode and finally calculating the grand average of the mean activity $\bar{v}_j(t) = \sum_{d=1}^{k} v_j^d(t)/50$ associated to each electrode and all k decisions (Figure 5.8). Now, it is possible to identify specific EEG components of the grand average $\bar{v}(t) = \sum_{i=1}^{20} \bar{v}_i(t)/20$ of all 20 electrodes associated with the different subtasks required to select the stock, set the price and quantity and finally defining the type of transactions. These ERA components are defined by the positive or negative (maximum or minimum) mean values of the recorded electrical field and the time they occur. For example, ERA component associated with stock selection is composed by three positive peaks approximately around 1,800, 1,600 and 1,500 ms before OK was pressed (Figure 5.8). Quantity ERA component begun as a negative activity around 1,400 ms, reached a positive peak around 1,200 ms and ended as a negative activity

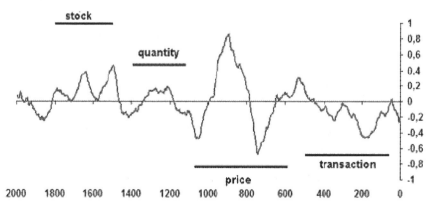

Figure 5.8 ERA associated with financial decision in the stock market game simulation.

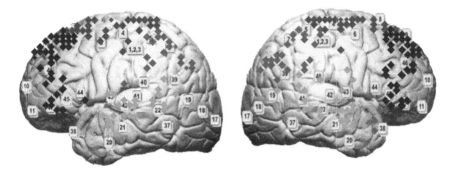

Figure 5.9 LORETA identification of cortical areas activated during the stock market game simulation.

around 1,000 ms. The most prominent ERA component is associated to pricing stock to be traded.

5.3.2 Low resolution tomography (LORETA) analysis

LORETA uses measurements of scalp electric potential differences $(v_i(t))$ to find the 3D distribution of the generating electric neuronal activity, with exact zero error localization to point-test sources (Pasqual-Marqui, 2002a,b). This technique has been widely used in studies covering very different aspects of brain physiology and it allows for identification of the sets of cortical neurons (s_l) activated during a cognitive task processing. Figure 5.9 shows the different cortical sources of electrical activity associated with the grand average $\bar{v}(t)$ shown in Figure 5.8. Only those sources associated to statistically significant $\bar{v}(t)$ are shown (Z score greater than 1.91).

5.4 Statistical Techniques to Analyze EEG Data

5.4.1 Quantifying the amount of information provided by each electrode

As discussed above, $v_i(t)$ recorded from a single electrode e_i is a simple weighted w_i sum of underlying k cortical source signals s_l that are active at time t. In this context, the correlation coefficient $r_{i,j}$ calculated between the activities $v_i(t)$, $v_j(t)$ recorded by e_i, e_j is expected to be highly dependent on the w_i^l, w_j^l weights determining the contribution of s_l to these recorded activities. If w_i^l, w_j^l are high, then source s_l is an important determinant of both $v_i(t)$ and $v_j(t)$ increasing the determination coefficient $r_{i,j}$ whenever it is active. If two different sources s_l, s_m are influential upon e_i, e_j, respectively, then $r_{i,j}$ approaches 1 or -1 if they are positively or negatively correlated. In this context, the determination coefficient $|r_{i,j}|$ increases if s_l, s_m are either near to both e_i, e_j or are synchronized. In contrast, if all sources that are influential upon $v_i(t), v_j(t)$ are silent, then $|r_{i,j}|$ approaches 0.5. In this theoretical context, the highest uncertainty about the information provided by e_i, e_j about s_l and s_m occurs when $|r_{i,j}|$ approaches 0.5, and it is $v_i(t), v_j(t)$ when $|r_{i,j}|$ approaches 1. Because of that, Rocha *et al.* (2005, 2010, 2011, 2013) proposed that $H(e_i)$ provided by e_i about the sources s_l is the expected entropy value $E(I(r_{i,j}))$ of the information $I(r_{i,j})$ provided by $|r_{i,j}|$ (Shannon, 1948) (see Methods for further details).

$H(e_i)$[1] calculated for each decision-making may be averaged $\bar{H}(e_i)$ according to subtasks, experimental groups, gender and any other parameter. Color coding is used to build $\bar{H}(e_i)$ brain mappings characterizing brain activity according to the chosen classification. In addition, it is possible to calculate differences between $\bar{H}(e_i)$ obtained for each gender to characterize the possible gender reasoning differences. Figure 5.10 shows examples of $\bar{H}(e_i)$ mappings.

5.4.2 Factor analysis

Factor analysis (FA)[2] may be used to study $H(e_i)$ covariation promoted by the coordinate activity of neurons belonging to the distinct neural systems involved in trading decisions. FA mappings of brain activity were computed taking into consideration the loading factors $f_j(e_i)$ of each electrode e_i on each FA pattern P_j. FA mappings are proposed to represent the activity of the neural circuits enrolled in a cognitive task because they condense the information provided by the electrodes sampling this neural activity. In this case, FA does not

---

[1] $H(e_i)$ calculation is discussed in detail in Chapter 10.
[2] Factor analysis is discussed in detail in Chapter 10.

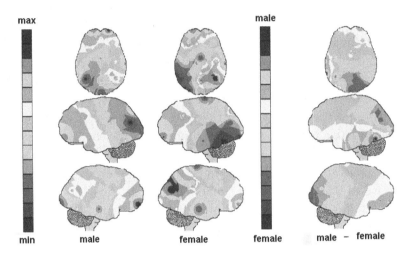

Figure 5.10 Entropy EEG mappings calculated for male, female and the difference between gender.

map brain areas activated by a cognitive task, but rather it provides information to disclose the activity of circuits composed by neurons distributed on different areas of the brain recruited by a cognitive task. FA mappings associated with trading in the stock market are shown in Figure 5.11 and shows that $H(e_i)$ covaried according to three different patterns. The first one is composed mostly by the frontal electrodes; the second one is composed by temporal and parietal electrodes and the last one by the occipital electrodes.

Combining LORETA and FA analyses, it is possible to disclose the cortical areas associated with each FA pattern, and therefore, enrolled in specific circuits in charge of solving the different subtasks required for trading decision.

5.4.3   Linear discriminant analysis

Linear discriminant analysis (LDA)[3] may be used to study $H(e_i)$ sample group variations. LDA is specifically useful in situations where the spreads of these variations might overlap and consequently must not be described simply by the loadings of the dimension represented

---

[3]LDA is discussed in detail in Chapter 10.

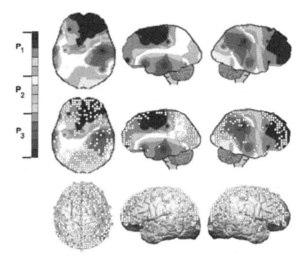

Figure 5.11 FA brain mappings (upper mappings) and associated cortical activity as revealed by LORETA analysis (middle and inferior mappings).

by the difference between their corresponding means only. In other words, LDA mappings are proposed to extract the discriminant activity of the neural circuits enrolled in a cognitive task because they separate samples of distinct groups by maximizing their between-class variability, while minimizing their within-class variability.

LDA mappings might disclose, for instance, discriminant patterns between male and female sample groups, as shown in Figure 5.13 from top left to bottom right, grouping distinct cortical regions that mostly separate gender differences promoted by the coordinate activity of neurons belonging to the neural systems involved in trading decisions. They assume that the spreads of the sample groups follow a Gaussian distribution on generating the brain mappings.

5.4.4 Multiple regression analysis

Multiple regression analysis may be used to study correlations between financial variables and $H(e_i)$. Regression mappings as in Figure 5.13 are built color coding the statistically beta coefficients calculated for each electrode e_i. Those beta coefficients that are not statistically significant are color coded as zero. Mappings in

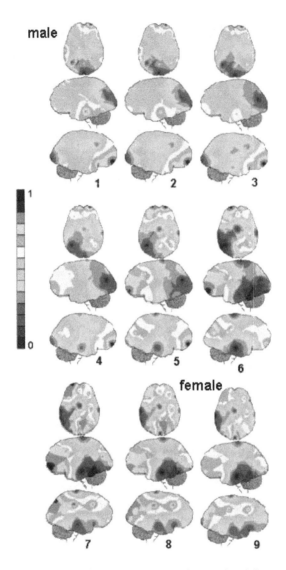

Figure 5.12 LDA brain mappings for gender differences.

Figure 5.12 correlate stock volatility and $H(e_i)$. Combining multiple regression and LORETA analyses allows for the identification of those cortical areas that are positive and negatively associated with the financial variable being studied (volatility in Figure 5.13).

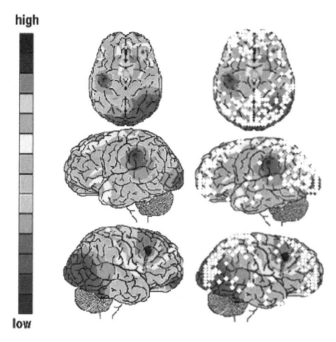

Figure 5.13 Regression brain mappings showing cortical areas involved in volatility analysis (left) as disclosed by LORETA analysis (right).

5.5 Comparing fMRI and EEG

The most popular difference that is cited in the literature between fMRI and EEG is that fMRI has the best spatial resolution and EEG has the best temporal discrimination. This is because fMRI is dependent on vascular alteration induced by local cellular activity that occurs in the range of seconds, whereas EEG records electrical activity with a temporal resolution that depends on the sampling frequency that is usually 256 Hz. This is also because EEG records cortical activity and its spatial resolution depends on the number of recording electrodes that is usually 20 and at most 124 and it records only cortical activity, whereas fMRI resolution depends on the size of voxel and the number of slices that are recorded that have been improved as the size of used high magnetic fields and it may scan subcortical besides cortical activities.

However, from our point of view, subtraction paradigm in fMRI limits its usefulness in financial decision-making, despite the fact that fMRI is by far the most used technique for such a purpose. Subtraction paradigm has two important drawbacks. First, it assumes that brain activity is a linear function of any given behavioral variable. Second, it restricts the number of variables that may be studied in contrast to EGG, as in the examples provided in this chapter.

For these reasons, we have been used EEG instead of fMRI in our studies on financial decision and we will further provide information about EEG use for such a purpose in the remainder of this book.

References

Bland, A., Schaefer, A. (2011). Electrophysiological correlates of decision making under varying levels of uncertainty. *Brain Research*, 1417, 55–66.

Breiter, H., Aharon, I., Kahneman, D., Dale, A., Shizgal, P. (2001). Functional imaging of neural responses to expectancy and experience of monetary gains and losses. *Neuron*, 30, 619–639.

Burgess, P., Gonen-Yaacovi, G., Volle, E. (2011). Functional neuroimaging studies of prospective memory: What have we learnt so far? *Neuropsychologia*, 49, 2246–2257.

Cohen, M., Elger, C., Ranganat, C. (2007). Reward expectation modulates feedback-related negativity and EEG spectra. *NeuroImage*, 35, 968–978.

Cohen, M., Ridderinkhof, K., Haupt, S., Elger, C., Fell, J. (2008). Medial frontal cortex and response conflict: Evidence from human intracranial EEG and medial frontal cortex lesion. *Brain Research*, 1238(31), 127–142.

Davis, C., Hauf, J., Wu, D., Everhart, D. (2011). Brain function with complex decision making using electroencephalography. *International Journal of Psychophysiology*, 79, 175–183.

FitzGerald, T., Seymour, B., Bach, D., Dolan, R. (2010). Differentiable neural substrates for learned and described value and risk. *Current Biology*, 20, 1823–1829.

Gehring, W., Willoughby, J. (2002). The medial frontal cortex and the rapid processing of monetary gains and losses. *Science*, 295, 2279–2282.

Knutson, B., Fong, G., Bennett, S., Adams, C., Hommer, D. (2003). A region of mesial prefrontal cortex tracks monetarily rewarding outcomes: Characterization with rapid event-related FMRI. *NeuroImage*, 18, 263–272.

Knutson, B., Taylor, J., Kaufman, M., Peterson, R., Glover, G. (2005). Distributed neural representation of expected value. *Journal of Neuroscience*, 25, 4806–4812.

Kuhnen, C., Knutson, B. (2005). The neural basis of financial risk taking. *Neuron*, 47, 763–770.

Knutson, B., Bossaerts, P. (2007). Neural antecedents of financial decisions. *Journal of Neuroscience*, 27, 8174–8177.

Knutson, B. (2007). Anticipation of monetary gain but not loss in older adults. *Nature Neuroscience*, 10, 787–791.

Knutson, B., Rick, S., Wimmer, G., Prelec, D., Loewenstein, G. (2007). Neural predictors of purchases. *Neuron*, 53, 147–156.

McClure, E., Monk, C., Nelson, E., Zarahn, E., Leibenluft, E., Bilder, R., Charney, D., Ernst, M., Pine, D. (2004). A developmental examination of gender differences in brain engagement during evaluation of threat. *Biology Psychiatry*, 55(11), 1047–1055.

Pascual-Marqui, R., Esslen, M., Kochi, K., Lehmann, D. (2002a). Functional imaging with low resolution brain electromagnetic tomography (LORETA): a review. *Methods & Findings in Experimental & Clinical Pharmacology*, 24C, 91–95.

Pascual-Marqui, R. (2002b). Standardized low resolution brain electromagnetic tomography (sLORETA): technical details. *Methods & Findings in Experimental & Clinical Pharmacology*, 24D, 5–12.

Polezzi, D., Sartori, G., Rumiati R., Vidotto, G., Daum, I. (2010). Brain correlates of risky decision-making. *NeuroImage*, 49, 1886–1894.

Preuschoff, K., Bossaerts, P., Quartz, S. (2006). Neural differentiation of expected reward and risk in human subcortical structures. *Neuron*, 51, 381–390.

Rocha, F. T., Rocha, A. F., Massad, E., Menezes, R. (2005). Brain mappings of the arithmetic processing in children and adults. *Cognitive Brain Res.* 22, 359–372 .

Rocha, A. F., Rocha, F. T., Massad, E., Burattini, M. N. (2010). Neurodynamics of an election. *Brain Research* 1351, 198–211.

Rocha, A. F., Rocha, F. T., Massad, E. (2011). The brain as a distributed intelligent processing system: an EEG study. *PLoS ONE* 6(3), e17355. doi:10.1371/journal.pone.0017355

Rocha, A. F., Rocha, F. T., Massad, E. (2013). Moral dilemma judgment revisited: a Loreta Analysis. *Journal of Behavioral and Brain Science*, doi: 10.4236/jbbs.2013.38066

Samanez-Larkin, G., Kuhnen, C., Yoo, D., Knutson, B. (2010). Variability in Nucleus Accumbens activity mediates age-related suboptimal financial risk taking. *Journal of Neuroscience*, 30, 1426–1434.

Seymour, B., McClure, S. (2008). Anchors, scales and the relative coding of value in the brain. *Current Opinion in Neurobiology*, 18, 173–178.

Shannon, C. E. (1948). A mathematical theory of communication. *The Bell System Technical Journal*, 27, 379–423.

Tobler, P., Fletcher, C., Bullmore, E., Schultz, W. (2007). Learning-related human brain activations reflecting individual finances. *Neuron*, 54, 167–175.

Chapter 6

How to Make an Experiment with EEG

The purpose of this chapter is to explain for starters, step by step, how they can create an experiment in social science area using Electroencephalogram (EEG) technology.

6.1 Type of Experiment

One of the first main decisions to be made is to choose between a controlled or an ecological experiment:

Well-Controlled Experiment: in this type of study, the researcher has the entire control of the variables supposed to support the decision-making process, because the environmental conditions are manipulated. It is the most common experimental paradigm in the literature (Blander and Schaefer, 2011; Fitzgerald *et al.*, 2010; Kuhnen and Knutson, 2005; Knutson *et al.*, 2007; Sanfey *et al.*, 2003, among several others). In this kind of experiment, a game is designed that permits the entire control of the variables of interest. The study determines how these variables are manipulated to show how brain activity is influenced by them in the decision-making process. Some of these games are very popular in the literature, such as the Ultimatum and Prisoner's Dilemma Games used to study cooperation or competition among people in decision-making (Grecucci *et al.*, 2013; Rilling *et al.*, 2004).

Ecological Experiment: in this type of study, real data is used to investigate decision-making, which reduces the capacity of the researcher to control the experiment, but allows for a more ecological approach of the process. It is the approach that we use in this chapter to discuss experimental planning. Once the subject of investigation is defined, the researcher has to obtain real data that may be used in the experiment, allowing some control of the variables or to design a set of questions about the subject of interest.

6.2 Designing Software to Make a Decision-making Simulation

Once the type of experiment is selected, specific software has to be developed to create the scenario for decision-making.

Some studies may require sophisticated software as the stock game simulator developed by Vieito *et al.* (2013) and Rocha *et al.* (2015) to study trading decision-making as described in Chapter 8. Screens of this software display financial information about stocks of seven different companies so that volunteers have to decide about holding the portfolio unchanged or select a company to sell or buy a specified amount of stocks at a given price Figure 8.1 — Chapter 8. Whenever a decision is made, the OK button is pressed.

Some other studies may require simple software to display specific screens with the different questions to be answered as in the case of dilemma studies (Chapter 9), or distinct blocks of screens to study decision-making and their motivation as in the case of Vote decision discussed in Chapter 10.

Specific buttons in these screens must be assigned allowing the volunteer to move from one screen to another and/or to select options to express his/her decision.

An important function of the developed software is to save information about the pressed buttons and their timing response.

6.3 Using EEG

There are many different types of EEG recording systems available in the market, which vary mostly according to the number of electrodes

e_i used to record the electrical cortical activity $v(e_i, t)$, frequency of data acquisition and resolution. The minimum requirements for an acceptable EEG recording system are 20 electrodes, 256 Hz for data acquisition and 16 bits for data resolution. The remaining comments in this chapter assume this type of EEG recording system.

Nowadays, there exist many different devices that allow electrodes to be easily and adequately placed over the skull, independent of their numbers.

Two laptops have to be used to run the experiment (Figure 6.1). One of them is in charge of the running EEG acquisition and the other to run the decision-making software discussed above. The clocks of both computers are synchronized.

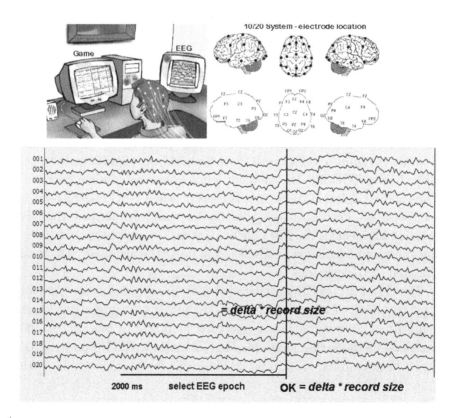

Figure 6.1 EEG recording session.

Table 6.1   An example of synchronization table.

Action	Time	Delta
Start	14:33:23	
New screen	14:33:38	15
OK pressing	14:33:23	55
New screen	14:33:23	70
OK pressing	14:33:23	100
New screen	14:33:23	115
OK pressing	14:33:23	150
New screen	14:33:23	165
OK pressing	14:33:23	210
New screen	14:33:23	225
OK pressing	14:33:23	250
New screen	14:33:23	265
OK pressing	14:33:23	320

Whenever a new screen is displayed, for example, in the stock trading game, the corresponding time on its clock is saved together with the information *New Screen*, and whenever the OK button is pressed, signalizing decision-making, the corresponding time is saved together with the information *OK button pressing* (see Table 6.1). Because the laptop's clocks are synchronized, it is possible to localize, later, in the EEG file, the moment when volunteer made a decision. The value of *delta* (in Table 6.1) is used to select EEG epochs associated with the decision-making for further analysis, because the OK pressing moment in the EEG file is identified by multiplying *delta* by the size of the record (*record size*) containing the acquired data from the used (20) electrodes.

Epochs of 2 s[1] of EEG activity ($v(e_i, t)$) are selected before and/or after the event of interest (e.g., the OK button pressing in the stock game as in Figure 6.1), each one corresponding to one of the 100 decisions made during game playing. The select EEG data is saved on *txt* files, each file containing 20 lines (one for each electrode) with

---

[1]According Rocha *et al.* (2013), the 2 s before is the moment when the brain makes the decision.

512 $v(e_i, t)$ measurements corresponding to the EEG sampled at the rate of 256 Hz during the selected 2 s.

6.4 Analysis of the EEG Data Quality

While playing the game, volunteer is prone to make spontaneous movements other than those involved in the requested typing of decision-making. If these movements are important, they will add important noise to the EGG recording. So, in this way, it is necessary to visually inspect the recorded EEG to eliminate the bad records, mostly in the case of those restless volunteers.

Automatic filters may be used to correct or to eliminate those sporadic bad EEG epochs that may be present in acceptable recorded EEG. Here, calculated $H(e_i)$ is used for such a purpose. The rationality is the following.

External noise, in general, affect recording by all (or at most all) electrodes. Because of that, external noise increases determination coefficient $r_{i,j}$ between all electrodes and drastically decreases $H(e_i)$ calculated for all electrodes e_i such that $\sum_i^{20} H(e_i)$ approaches 0. Here, all EEG epochs resulting in $\sum_i^{20} H(e_i) < 1$ were eliminated from further analysis.

6.5 Tools used for EEG Analysis

Because EEG data are assumed to be a weighted sum of the electrical activity of different sources s_l, correlation analysis of the electrical activity $v(e_i, t)$ recorded by the different electrodes e_i may be used to summarize information provided by each electrode e_i about all involved sources s_i into a single variable as proposed by Foz *et al.* (2002) and Rocha *et al.* (2010, 2011, 2013, 2015). The rationality is the following. In this context, the amount of information $H(e_i)$ provided by electrode e_i about the sources s_l is assumed to be a function of the determination coefficient of the correlation $r_{i,j}$ between $v(e_i, t)$ and $v(e_j, t)$.[2]

---

[2]See Chapter 5 for more details.

Using N, recording electrodes demands computation of N^2 correlations between the recorded activities to calculate $H(e_i)$. In the case of 20 electrodes, $H(e_i)$ calculation demands computation of 400 correlations for each EEG epoch selected for analysis. If instead of an EEG equipment with 20 electrodes, we use an equipment with 32 electrodes, the number of required correlations to estimate $H(e_i)$ would be of 384,204,800, increasingly drastically the need of computing power and time.

LORETA software uses the *txt* files of the selected EEG data to identify the sources s_l that possibly contribute to the generation of the recorded electrical field $v(e_j, t)$. It is possible, therefore, to identify these sources for each selected EEG epoch for each decision-making and for each experimental group. However, LORETA analysis of each isolated selected EEG epoch is practically meaningless.

It has been showed that LORETA spatial power discrimination increases with the number of recording electrodes. However, Mitchel *et al.* (2004) have shown that a minimum of well-distributed 19 electrodes are required for LORETA analysis.

Factor analysis (FA) is a statistical tool to investigate patterns of covariation in a large number of variables and to determine whether information may be condensed into small sets of these variables called principal components. This transformation is defined in such a way that the first principal component is the one that accounts for as much of the variability in the data as possible, and each succeeding component in turn explains the subsequent amount of possible variance under the constraint that is orthogonal to (i.e., uncorrelated with) the preceding components. Contribution of each variable $f_j(v)$ to each covariation principal component P_j disclosed by FA is named loading factor $f_j(v)$ on P_j.

FA may be applied to study the covariation of $H(e_i)$ during decision-making. FA mappings of brain activity were computed taking into consideration the loading factors $f_j(e_i)$ of each electrode e_i on each P_j. FA mappings are proposed to represent the activity of the neural circuits enrolled in a cognitive task because they condense the information provided by the electrodes sampling this neural activity. In this case, FA does not map brain areas activated by a cognitive task, but rather, it provides information to disclose the activity of circuits composed by neurons distributed on different areas of the brain recruited by a cognitive task.

There is no statistical rule to select relevant electrodes taking into consideration their loading values $f_j(v)$. Here, we select those electrodes having $f_j(v) > 0.5$ to construct FA mappings characterizing each identified principal component P_j. FA is used either as a prospective or retrospective analysis. Prospective analysis is applied when no previous information is available about the covariation of a set of variables, in order to provide a first identification of possible FA components. After this first analysis, FA is used prospectively to verify how adequate these components are to study a given problem.

Multiple linear regression analysis may be used to estimate the function $v = \tau + \sum_{i=1}^{20} \beta_i h(e_i)$ correlating any variable of interest v and the net entropy $h(e_i)$. Statistical inference logic is based on rejecting the null hypotheses whenever likelihood of the observed data under the null hypotheses is low. The likelihood of witnessing a rare event also increases with the number of used electrodes and this augments the chance to reject a null hypothesis when it is true. There exist many statistical methods to counteract this problem. The most used one is Bonferroni method (Bonferroni, 1936) that specifies the threshold for statistical significance for each statistical inference.

6.5.1 EEG average and grand average

The first step in this analysis is to obtain the average $(\bar{v}(e_i, t))$ EEG data collected for the K decisions made by each experimental group, that is to say to average the values of $v_n^d(e_i, t)$ acquired for each (n) of the G volunteers and each of his/her decision d, according to (Figure 6.1)

$$\bar{v}(e_i, t) = \sum_{n=1}^{G} \sum_{d=1}^{K} v_n^d(e_i, t). \tag{6.1}$$

The averaged EEG for each experimental group (groups G_1 and G_2 in Chapter 8) or phase (e.g., phases F, A and D in Chapter 9) are saved in the *Average EEG spreadsheets* (Figure 6.2).

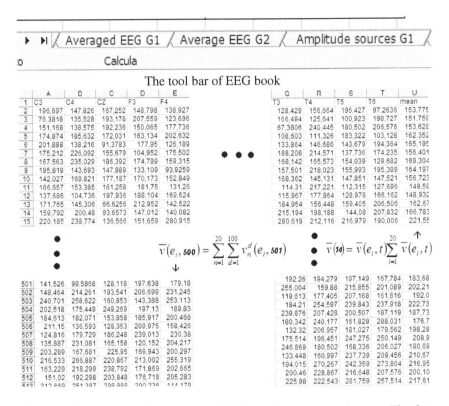

Figure 6.2 Averaging the recorded EEG for each experimental group. The data is shown in spreadsheets *EEG averages*.

Another useful average is the so-called *Grand Average* $\bar{v}(t)$ that is calculated by averaging the electrode mean values calculated for each electrode (Figure 6.3) according to

$$\bar{v}(t) = \sum_{i=1}^{20} \bar{v}(e_i, t). \tag{6.2}$$

*Grand Average*s are calculated in the spreadsheets *Averaged EEG* (Figure 6.2). The graphics of these Grand Averages are shown (Figure 6.3) in the spreadsheets *EEG components* and *Summary LORETA*.

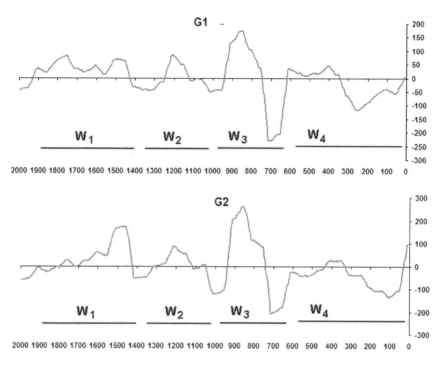

Figure 6.3 Grand averages and EEG waves calculated for groups G_1 and G_2.

It may be observed (in Figure 6.3) that four clear EEG waves are identified for both G_1 and G_2 beginning around 1,700, 1,300, 1,000 and 600 ms before the OK button was pressed. Similar components are also observed in the other EEG books.

Trading decision-making required selection of a stock and decisions about quantity, and price and transaction (sell or buy) before pressing the OK button (see Figure 8.1). It is possible that the waves identified in the *Grand Averages* are related with these events. Decision about holding portfolio unaltered just required pressing the OK button, but *holding* corresponds to only 20% of the decisions. And even in these cases, it is possible that volunteers have thought at least about stocks, prices and quantities.

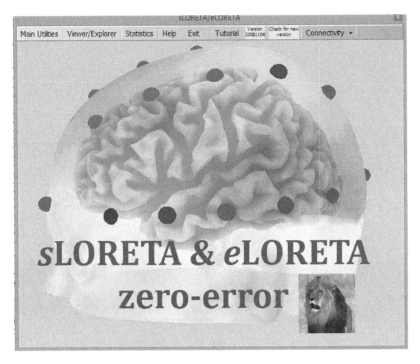

Figure 6.4 LORETA software. LORETA window to calculate average EEG files.

6.5.2   Using **LORETA**

6.5.2.1   *Identifying amplitude sources*

Data from spreadsheets *Averaged EEG* are used to identify the possible electrical sources s_l or sets of cortical neurons that contributed to generate the recorded electrical field $v(e_i, t)$ while volunteers were playing the game. For this purpose, data on these spreadsheets have to be exported as *txt* files.

Viewer/Explore window was selected and one *txt* file was loaded using *FileExplorer* function (Figure 6.4). This function was also used to load the file *eletrodos.spinv* with electrode coordinates (extension spinv[3]). In the sequence, you provide information about electrodes

---

[3]If you are using 20 electrodes, you may download the file eletrodos.spinv used here at (local).

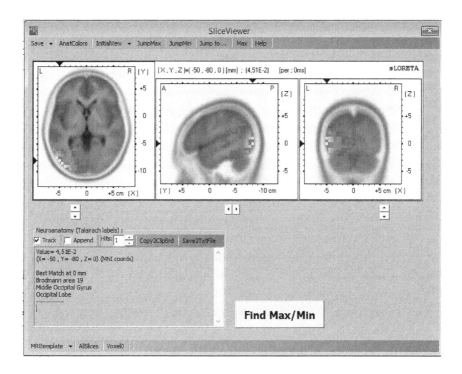

Figure 6.5 LORETA window showing identified sources.

(20) and sample rate (256 Hz) and the windows in Figures 6.5 and 6.6 will be shown.

LORETA provides information about the Brodmann area and the anatomic structure of each identified LORETA source (ILS), besides the X, Y, Z coordinates of the first and most important solution. But you may select up to four other alternative solutions, by specifying the number of hits in the *SlicerViewer* (Figure 6.5) screen. Here, three hits were used.

Moving the cursor over the EEG displayed in the *EEG/ERP signals* window makes the software to calculate the possible sources for the amplitudes marked by the cursor. It is possible to save information about the identified sources by selecting buttons *track* and *append* in SliceViewer window (Figure 6.6) and selecting either the clipboard or a file to save data. The format of the information you get is shown in Figure 6.1.

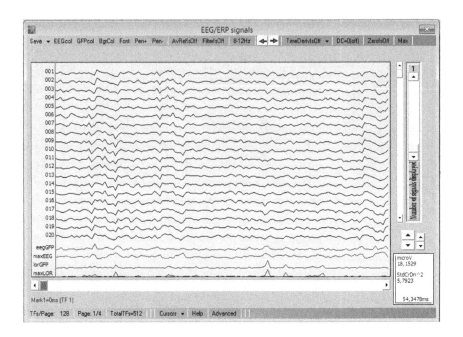

Figure 6.6 EEG/ERP signals.

In this format, information provided by LORETA is not very useful and it is necessary to convert it, for example, to the format used in spreadsheets *Amplitude LORETA sources*. The *converter* used here is in spreadsheet *LORETA decoder*. LORETA output (Figure 6.1) is pasted in the column *LORETA output* and copy columns *X* to *Lobe3* and paste it on the corresponding spreadsheet *Amplitude LORETA source*. The decoder spreadsheet is programmed to handle only 128 samples such that the process has to be repeated four times to cover EEG epochs of 512 samples as used in this book. Columns BA_i, $Anatomy_i$ and $Lobe_i$ correspond to the three chosen LORETA solutions.

A code combining both BA number and anatomical location is presented in the spreadsheet *Parameters*. This code with 113 possible ILS locations was created with the results of using LORETA by our group to study EEG activity of more than 700 people making around 20,000 decisions on different subjects (Arruda *et al.*, 2008; Foz *et al.*,

2002; Ribas *et al.*, 2013; Rocha *et al.*, 2005, 2011, 2013, 2014a,b, 2015).

Spreadsheet *Amplitude source frequencies* shows the frequencies of location of ILSs identified as first solution according to this code.

Graphics in spreadsheet *Amplitude source mappings* show the XYZ locations for ILSs associated with decision-making. Superposition of graphics showing the left and right sagittal views of the brain may show that differences on ILS location between groups or decision phases are being studied.

6.5.2.2 *Identifying band frequency sources*

Information (spike trains) arriving into a given cortical area promotes local electrical activity at the synapses that are either depolarization (the cell inside becomes positively charged in relation to its exterior) or hyper polarization (the cell inside becomes more negatively charged in relation to its exterior) that outlast incoming information (see Chapter 3). The postsynaptic activity triggered by presynaptic information is reflected in the actual value $V(e_i, t)$ recorded by e_i and LORETA identify it in the EEG amplitude analysis. Postsynaptic activity outlasts the presynaptic incoming information for a period of time that is variables for different cortical cells and they are important sources of the different band frequencies identified in $v(e_i, t)$ by means of the fast Fourier Transform (FFT). It may be said that different *memory* copies of the incoming information remains in these different time evolutions of the postsynaptic activity.

FFT decomposes the recorded EEG into a voltage by frequency spectral graph commonly called the "power spectrum", with power being the square of the EEG magnitude, and magnitude being the integral average of the amplitude of the EEG signal, measured from + peak to − peak, across the time sampled (e.g., Cohen, 1995). Typically, the EEG is decomposed into sinusoidal series within the following frequency bands:

- Delta band: comprising frequencies smaller than 4 Hz.
- Theta band: comprising frequencies between 4 and 7 Hz.

- Alpha band: comprising frequencies between 8 and 15 Hz.
- Beta band: comprising frequencies between 16 and 30 Hz.
- Gamma band: comprising frequencies above 30 Hz.

It must be kept in mind that band boundaries may vary from author to author.

FFT is calculated for a given time window that, in general, is set for the entire window of the studied EEG epoch. However, it is possible to use it for small windows. In this case, it is possible to calculate what is called time-varying cross spectra (TVSCR) by moving the window throughout the entire EEG epoch. There is no specific rule to determine the size of this window; here, its duration was set *ad hoc* to 50 ms.

LORETA allows you to calculate TVSCR and to locate the possible sources generating each studied frequency. To do this, you have to first calculate the TVSCR for the averaged EEG in the selected epoch. In the present case, TVSCR was calculated using data on spreadsheets *Averaged EEG*. For such purpose, MainUtilities window was chosen and *TVSCR* function in this utility was selected. The following information is requested for TVSCR processing: the *txt* file containing the EEG data; number of electrodes (e.g., 20); number of sample points (e.g., 512); sampling rate (256 Hz); frequency boundaries of band to be studied (e.g., 0–64); window width (e.g., 50) and the name and the place to save file (extension tvcrss) that is created to same results.

Once the *tvcrss* is created, *slor* files for each of the frequencies to be studied have to be calculated. This is done by selecting the function *TVSCR to sLORETA* to create each desired *slor* file. To do this, the following information is requested: *tvcrss* and *spinv* files. In the sequence, it is necessary to select the button *Single frequency* and the frequency of interest.

Finally, to identify the sources generating the different frequencies of interest, the ViewExplorer utility has to be used as described above (7.6.2) to identify the sources associated with each frequency. The difference is that now it is necessary to select the corresponding *slor* file to generate the file containing LORETA description of the identified sources (Figure 6.1).

Using the spreadsheet *LORETA decoder* and the spreadsheet *Data encoder*, it is possible to create the temporal lists of ILS for each studied frequency as those in spreadsheet *Band frequencies LORETA sources*. Paste LORETA output (e.g., Figure 6.1) on *LORETA decoder* spreadsheet and move results to *Data encoder* spreadsheet. As explained to this, four times to process 512 $v(e_i, t)$ samples for each studied frequency. In the sequence, copy columns *source to zd* from *Data encoder* spreadsheet to the same columns of *Band frequencies LORETA sources* spreadsheet. Starting with frequency 1 Hz, past these data on lines $2, 2 + 512, 2 + 1024, \ldots$ for each studied frequency. Data must be pasted at columns C, AN, etc. depending on the number of studied groups and/or decision phases.

Here, ILSs were calculated for the following frequencies 1, 2, 3, 4, 5, 6, 7, 8, 9, 10, 11, 12, 13, 15, 20, 30, 40, 50 and 60, and data were sequentially pasted in the spreadsheet *Band frequencies mappings* according to this sequence.

Spatial location of ILS computed for G_1 and G_2 are shown in the spreadsheets *Source Band mappings* and *Summary LORETA* for theta, delta, alpha, beta and gamma bands.

6.5.3 Multivariate analysis

EEG txt files containing acquired data $v(e_i, t)$ for each selected EEG epoch are used to calculate the amount of information $H(e_i)$ that are saved in a *xls* file, where columns are specified for each of the 20 used electrodes and lines contain $H(e_i)$ calculated values for each selected epoch. Behavioral data have to be adequately merged to this *xls* file.

The *entropy.xls* file described above is used for FA, linear discriminating analysis, logistic and multilinear regression analyses. For this purpose, any commercial software or in-house developed routines may be used.

The results of these analyses have to be formatted to allow for data to be pasted in the corresponding yellow areas of the spreadsheets *FA mappings*, *LDA mappings*, *Logistic Regression* and *MRL* spreadsheets.

FA, in general, reveals three different patterns having eigenvalues greater than 1 and explaining around 80% of $H(e_i)$ covariation

(Foz *et al.*, 2002; Rocha *et al.*, 2010, 2013, 2014a,b, 2015). The loading factors for the different electrodes range in the interval $(0, 1)$. There is no formal criterion to classify loading factors as significant or not. Here, *FA mappings* include electrodes having loadings greater than 0.5.

FA is used as either a prospective or retrospective tool. Initially, when there is no previous information about covariation of the studied variable, FA results are used as potential explanation about the studied phenomenon. As new studies continue to confirming previous results, FA becomes a tool for retrospective analysis and explanation it provides start to be used as confirmation of initial hypothesis about the studied phenomenon. This is the case of FA analysis about $H(e_i)$ covariation used in this book.

Statistical significance of inferences derived from logistic multilinear regression analyses is subject to specific rules, because inference logic is based on rejecting the null hypotheses if the likelihood of the observed data under the null hypotheses is low. As the number of hypotheses being tested increases the likelihood of a rare event also increases, and therefore, the likelihood of incorrectly rejecting a null hypothesis augments. This is the so-called Type 1 error in statistics. There are various methods to solve this problem by adjusting the significance threshold. The most common are Bonferroni and family-wise error rate (FWER) corrections. Bonferroni correction is the method used in this book.

References

Arruda, L., Rocha, F., Rocha, F. (2008). Studying the satisfaction of patients on the outcome of an aesthetic dermatological filler treatment. *Journal of Cosmetic Dermatology*, 7, 246–250.

Bland, A., Schaefer, A. (2011). Electrophysiological correlates of decision making under varying levels of uncertainty. *Brain Research*, 1417, 55–66.

Bonferroni, C. (1936). *Teoria Statistica Delle Classi e Calcolo Dele Probabilità.* Istituto Superiore di Science Economich e Comercialli di Firenzi, Italy.

Cohen, L. (1995). *Time–Frequency Analysis.* Prentice-Hall, New York.

FitzGerald, T., Seymour, B., Bach, D., Dolan, R. (2010). Differentiable neural substrates for learned and described value and risk. *Current Biology*, 20, 1823–1829.

Foz, F., Lucchini, F., Palimieri, S., Rocha, A., Rodella, E., Rondó, A., Cardoso, M., Ramazzini, P., Leite, C. (2002). Language plasticity revealed by EEG mapping. *Pediatric Neurology*, 26, 106–115.

Grecucci, A., Giorgetta, C., van't Wout, M., Bonini, N., Sanfey, A. (2013). Reappraising the ultimatum: An FMRI study of emotion regulation and decision making. *Cerebral Cortex*, 23, 399–410.

Knutson, B., Rick, G., Wimmer, E., Prelec, D., Loewenstein, G. (2007). Neural predictors of purchases. *Neuron*, 53, 147–156.

Kuhnen, C., Knuston, B. (2005). The neural basis of financial risk taking. *Neuron*, 47, 763–770.

Mitchel, C., Murray, M., Lantz, G., Gonzalez, S., Spinelli, L., Peralta, R. (2004). EEG source imaging. *Clinical Neurophysiology*, 115, 2195–2222.

Ribas, L., Rocha, F., Ortega, N., Rocha, A., Massad, E. (2013). Brain activity and medical diagnosis: An EEG study. *BMC Neuroscience*. doi:10.1186/1471-2202-14-109.

Rilling, J., Sanfey, A., Aronson, J., Nystrom, L., Cohen, J. (2004). The neural correlates of theory of mind within interpersonal interactions. *NeuroImage*, 22, 1694–1703.

Rocha, F., Rocha, A., Massad, E., Menezes, R. (2005). Brain mappings of the arithmetic processing in children and adults. *Cognitive Brain Research*, 22, 359–372.

Rocha, A., Rocha, F., Massad, E., Burattini, M. (2010). Neurodynamics of an election. *Brain Research*, 1351, 198–211.

Rocha, A., Rocha, F., Massad, E. (2011). The brain as a distributed intelligent processing system: An EEG study. *PLoS ONE*, 6(3), e17355.

Rocha, A., Rocha, F., Massad, E. (2013). Moral dilemma judgment revisited: A LORETA analysis. *Journal Behavioral and Brain Science*. doi:10.4236/jbbs.2013.38066.

Rocha, A., Massad, E., Rocha, F., Burattini, M. (2014a). Brain and law: An EEG study of how we decide or not to implement a law. *Journal of Behavioral and Brain Sciences*. http://dx.doi.org/10.4236/jbbs.2014.412054.

Rocha, F., Massad, E., Thomaz, C. (2014b). EEG brain mapping of normal and learning disabled children using factor and linear discriminant analyses. *Journal Neurophysiology*, 6(1). http://dx.doi.org/10.4172/2155-9562.1000262.

Rocha, A., Vieito, J., Massad, E., Rocha, F., Lima, R. (2015). Electroencephalographic activity associated to investment decision: Gender Difference. *Journal of Behavioral and Brain Sciences*, 5, 203–211. http://dx.doi.org/10.4236/jbbs.2015.56021.

Sanfey, A., Rilling, J., Aronson, J., Nystron, L., Cohen, J. (2003). The neural basis of economic decision-making in the ultimatum game. *Science*, 300, 1755–1758.

Vieito, J., Rocha, A.F., Rocha, F.T. (2013). Brain activity of the investor's stock market financial decision. *Journal of Behavioral Finance*, 16, 1–11. doi:10.1080/15427560.2015.1064931.

Chapter 7

Financial Decision-making

The purpose of this chapter is to discuss how to study financial decision-making in the stock market. Results that will be presented and discussed, here, are from a multinational study aimed to investigate brain activity associated with trading decision using a stock market game simulator. Electroencephalogram (EEG) is used to record brain activity and techniques discussed in Chapters 6 and 10 are used to analyze acquired data and results are interpreted assuming the brain as a distributed intelligent system (Chapter 4). Experiments were done in Brazil, the Netherlands and Portugal (Rocha *et al.*, 2015; Vieito *et al.*, 2015). Data selected from experiments in Portugal are available on *EEG_StockMarket* book that may be downloaded from http://www.eina.com.br/software/.

7.1 Designing Trading as an Ecological Game

As discussed in Chapter 6, an ecological approach of trading decision-making has to use real but controllable data. For such a purpose, prices $p(c, d)$ of stocks c traded at BMFBovespa[1] were collected from December 4, 2010, to December 30, 2012 (Rocha *et al.*, 2015; Vieito *et al.*, 2015). During this time interval, the Brazilian and other stock markets experienced distinct periods of volatility and price tendencies that characterized different periods of *Bull* or *Bear* markets. Careful selection of these periods allows for some control over variables of interest for financial decision, such as price evolution,

---

[1] www.bmfbovespa.com.br.

portfolio value, volatility, etc., while at the same time allowing the design of an ecological game simulating the real electronic stock trading.

Collected stock prices $p(c, d)$ were divided by the stock prices $p(c, 0)$ at January 4, 2010, to furnish the relative price index for each stock:

$$IND(c, d) = \frac{p(c, d)}{p(c, 0)}, \qquad (7.1)$$

for each trading day or trading decision d. Bourse indices $Index_{M_i}(d)$ were calculated as the average of $IND(c, d)$ (IND in Figure 7.1) for all seven companies (c) in each market.

$$Index_{M_i}(d) = \frac{\sum_{c=1}^{7} IND(c, d)}{7}, \qquad i = 1, 2, \qquad (7.2)$$

where $IND(c, d)$ is used to calculate the current trading stock value ($Value(d)$) in Figure 7.1) for 50 trading decisions in different types of marketing M_i by multiplying the corresponding $IND(c, d)$ by the stock value $p(c, e)$ in a day e before, but close to period planned to doing the experiment. Different types of M_i are created by selecting specific periods of 50 consecutive trading days from the general price database. Selection of these periods is guided by volatility, bourse crises, etc.

Company	IND	VAR	Value	Qt	TOTAL	T-Qt	Price	B	S
INDEX	0,96	-0,01							
BANIF	1,04	0,00	22,01	200	4.402,39		EU	⌀	⌀
Portugal Telecom	1,63	0,04	34,93	200	6.985,11		EU	⌀	⌀
Energias de Portugal	0,94	-0,00	20,90	200	4.180,35		EU	⌀	⌀
Banco Comercial Português	1,11	0,00	7,28	200	1.455,84		EU	⌀	⌀
BRISA	1,01	-0,01	31,70	200	6.340,69		EU	⌀	⌀
Cimentos de Portugal	1,00	-0,01	8,35	200	1.670,99		EU	⌀	⌀
Futebol Clube do Porto	0,98	0,03	35,85	200	7.170,95		EU	⌀	⌀
				Fb	32.206,31		OK		
A				**Pv**	31.670,00				
18.330,00				**C**	536,31				

Figure 7.1   The game screen.

Besides $IND(c, d)$, $Index_{M_i}(d)$ and $Value(d)$, the following pieces of information are made available to the volunteer for each trading decision d. The stock price variation ($Var(d)$) between consecutive trading screens were calculated and displayed; the number of stocks in the portfolio ($Qt(d)$); invested amounts $Total(c, d)$ on each stock c; portfolio's actual value ($Pv(c, d)$); total invested amount ($Fb(d)$), actual revenue or cash $C(d)$ and the available ($A(d)$) amount to new stock purchases.

IND is the relative stock price, VAR the difference between actual and previous relative stock price, $Value$ the actual real stock price, Qt the quantity of owned stocks, $Total$ the total invested in each stock, $T - Qt$ the proposed number of stocks to trade, $Price$ the proposed transaction price, S the selling option, B the buying option, OK to finish proposal. $Fb = Pv + C$; Pv the actual portfolio value, C the revenue (gain or loss) and A the available money for new tradings.

Trading simulation progressed as follows. While EGG is recorded, the volunteer digitizes number and price of a stock to trade for one and just one company and selected trading options B or S and pressed OK in order to sell or buy, respectively; or just pressed OK to maintain portfolio unaltered (see Figure 7.1). If price offer was within 5% variation of the next stock price ($p(c, d + 1)$), offer is accepted and the corresponding number of the selected stock adjusted; otherwise, offer is rejected and the corresponding number of the selected stock maintained is unaltered. After OK is pressed, a new screen is presented for another trading simulation ($d + 1$). This new screen shows updated information of the experimental variables.

Volunteers receive an initial portfolio of 200 shares of seven different companies to play the game by making 50 trading decisions taking into consideration data presented in each of the 50 game screens in each experimental session. By holding, selling or buying stocks, volunteers manipulate both their *portfoliovalue* and *cash* in the attempt to get *finalbalance = portfoliovalue + cash* greater than *marketvalue*. This may be accomplished by both increasing *portfoliovalue* and/or *cash*.

7.2   The Experimental Setting

Two laptops are used to run the experiment (see Figure 6.2). One of them is in charge of running EEG acquisition and the other to simulate the trading game. The clocks of both computers are synchronized. Whenever the OK button is pressed, the Game Software (GS) saves the corresponding time on its clock (see Table 6.1). Because the laptop clocks are synchronized, it is possible to localize, later, in the EEG file, the moment when volunteer made a decision. The value of *delta* (Table 6.1) is used to select EEG epochs associated with the decision-making for further analysis, because the OK pressing moment in the EEG file is identified by multiplying *delta* by the size of the record (*record size*) containing the acquired data from the used 20 electrodes.

Here, 100 EEG epochs of 2 s were selected before the OK button pressing (Figure 6.1), each one corresponding to one of the 100 decisions made during game play. Each experimental group G_1 and G_2 was composed by 20 volunteers, therefore 2,000 EEG epochs were saved on *txt* files, each file containing 20 lines (one for each electrode) with 512 $v(e_i, t)$ measurements corresponding to the EEG sampled at the rate of 256 Hz during the 2 s prior to OK button pressing.

A file in *txt* format saved the 512 $v(e_i, t)$ values sampled for each electrode e_i. This is done this way because Low resolution brain electromagnetic tomography available in Internet reads this type of file to average EEG data to be used to localize the possible cortical sources of the recorded EEG.

7.3   Population

Volunteers were 40 undergraduate students of the School of Business Studies from Polytechnic Institute of Viana do Castelo, Portugal, with no previous experience on the stock market. This guarantees that students were homogenous in terms of financial knowledge required to support trading decisions.

Two groups (G_1 and G_2) of 10 men and 10 women played the trading game simulating two different stock markets (M_1 and M_2). M_1 is a *bull market* in the period from May 31 to August 13, 2010, with prices steadily increasing and having low volatility M_2 corresponds to a transition from the previous bull market toward a *bear market* during March 21 to May 27. M_2 volatility was high with some stocks experiencing losses, while some others experiencing slow gains.

Group G_1 traded first (trading session S_1) on M_1 and later on M_2 (trading session S_2). In contrast, group G_2 traded first (S_1) on M_2 and later (S_2) on M_1. The stock price evolution in M_1 and M_2 are supposed to induce different financial behaviors and, consequently, brain activity associated with trading decisions is expected to be different.

7.4 EEG Components Identified in Grand Average

Inspection of graphics in Figure 7.2 (or spreadsheet *EEG components*) shows that four clear EEG waves are identified for both G_1

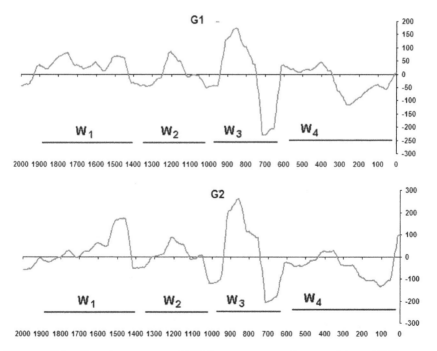

Figure 7.2 Grand averages and EEG waves as seen in spreadsheet *EEG components* and calculated for groups G_1 and G_2 from data on spreadsheets *Averaged EEG*.

and G_2 experimental groups beginning around 1,900, 1,350, 1,000 and 400 ms before the OK button was pressed (see time intervals in time window yellow cells in spreadsheet *Parameters*). Trading decision-making required first selecting a stock and then deciding about quantity, price and transaction (sell or buy) type before pressing the OK button. Therefore, it is possible to assume that the waves (W_1–W_4) identified in these plots are sequentially related to these decision events. Decision about holding portfolio unaltered just required pressing the OK button, but *holding* corresponds to only 20% of the decisions and even in these cases, it is possible that volunteers have thought at least about stocks, prices and quantities.

Linear regression analysis of Grand Averages (see Section 6.5.3.1) calculated for G_1 and G_2 shows that the two temporal series has a correlation of $R^2 = 0.7158$ (see graphic in spreadsheet *EEG components*) indicating that the identified EEG components may be considered similar, the major difference assigned to components W_1 and W_2.

7.5   Activated Cortical Areas

Figure 7.3 (see also spreadsheet *Summary* LORETA) shows the frequencies of location of identified LORETA sources (ILSs) identified as first solution for G_1 and G_2 according to the code listed in the spreadsheet *Parameters*.

ILSs predominated at BA 11 — Superior Frontal Gyrus; BA 17 and 18 — Cuneus; BA 18 — Middle Occipital Gyrus and BA 46 — Middle Frontal Gyrus in G_1 case, and they predominated at BA 5 — Postcentral Gyrus, all anatomical locations at BA 7 and 8, BA 10 — Middle Frontal Gyrus, BA 19 — Middle Occipital Gyrus and BA 21 — Middle Temporal Gyrus in G_2 case. Differences on ILS location between groups G_1 and G_2 predominated on the parietal and temporal lobes and over BA 44 as shown in G_1 and G_2.

It is possible to assume that because G_1 people begun to trade in the trendy market M_1, they learned that prices may be predictable and, perhaps, created linear models to project prices into future. This is easily done because it may take profit of neural circuits for carrying out multiplication (Rocha *et al.*, 2004, 2005). In such a context,

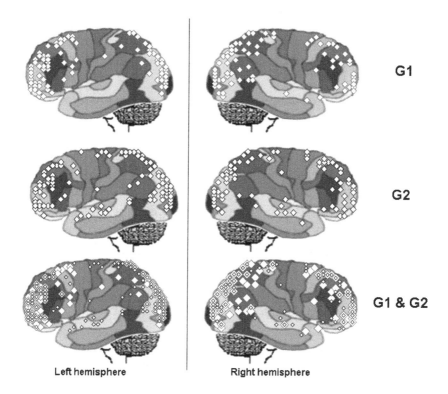

Figure 7.3 ILS spatial location as seen in *Summary LORETA* spreadsheet.

G_1 people would rely more on prospective expectations about prices (Rocha *et al.*, 2015). In this line of reasoning, G_1 people would use prospective reasoning to support their trading decisions. In contrast, G_2 people begun to trade in the volatile market M_2, then they may have learned that prices are unpredictable and, perhaps, relied more on present to past prices comparisons to reason retrospectively about market evolution and to make their decisions (Rocha *et al.*, 2015).

Boundaries to Area Subset 1 are set to 1 and 114 in the *EEG_StockMarket* book to select all identified sources to be displayed. But it is possible to select just one area to be studied by setting, for example, Subset 1 boundaries to 30 and 33 in order to select locations identified in BA 11 or boundaries may be set to 100 and 113 to select locations over the lateral frontal cortex. Addition of boundaries 22 and 40 for *Subset* 2 expands location of sources over the frontal cortex. Try boundaries 60 to 100 on *Subset* 1 letting the boundaries of the other subsets as 0, to discover that most of the differences on G_1 and G_2 reasoning depend on the activity at these areas.

The question to be answered by manipulation boundaries of area subsets is: Are hypotheses about prospective and retrospective reasoning supported by these results? What are the set of ILSs that differentiate reasoning by the two experimental groups? Search the literature for support to your conclusions.

Another analysis of data in *EEG_StockMarket* is to identify the cortical modules discussed in Chapter 4 that may be involved in the financial decision-making. The question to be answered is what are the modules that differentiate reasoning by the two experimental groups?

7.6   EEG Band Frequencies

The recorded EEG time-series may be decomposed into a set of senoidal time-series using, for example, fast Fourier transform (FFT) (see Chapter 6). LORETA decomposes the EEG in senoidal time-series of frequencies specified by users. Here ILSs were computed for theta, delta, alpha, beta and gamma bands. It must be remembered that this type of analysis provides additional information to that discussed in the previous section.

Spatial location of ILSs computed for G_1 and G_2 are shown in spreadsheets *Source Band mappings* and *Summary LORETA* for delta, theta, alpha, beta and gamma bands. It can be observed that locations varied for the different bands and experimental groups. For instance, locations of alpha sources at the left hemisphere quite distinguish experimental groups G_1 and G_2, because some of them are found at BA 22, 42, 40 and four in G_2 case but not in G_1 case (Figure 7.4).

Frequency of ILSs computed for G_1 and G_2 are shown in Figure 7.4 (or spreadsheet *Source Band frequencies*) and differed for these groups as shown in graphics G_1 and G_2. ILSs predominated in BA 17 — Cuneus, BA 18 and 19 — Middle Occipital Gyri in G_1

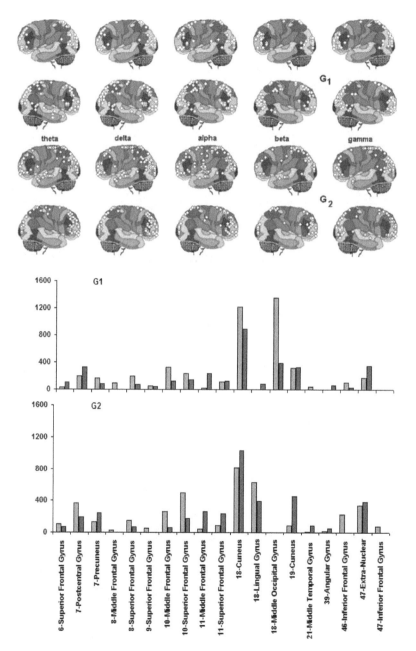

Figure 7.4 Spatial (upper mappings) and temporal (middle and low graphics) frequency ILS distributions.

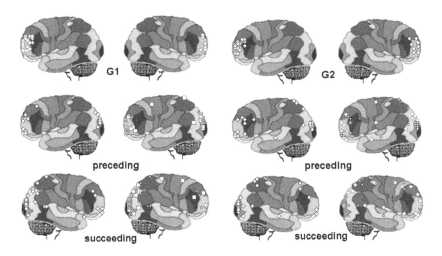

Figure 7.5 Locations of areas activated prior (preceding) and after (succeeding) activation of BA 11 for G_1 and G_2.

case, and they predominated in BA 7, BA 10 — Superior Frontal Gyrus, BA 28 — Lingual Gyrus and BA 19 — Precuneus in G_2 case.

7.7   Source Sequence

Figure 7.5 (or spreadsheet *Summary LORETA*) display, for both G_1 and G_2, the spatial location of the Brodmann areas that are identified by **LORETA** as activated previously and after the actual identified **LORETA** sources specified in spreadsheet *Parameters*. Figure 7.5 shows the results when BA 11 is selected by setting boundaries of *subset* 1 to 30 and 33.

It may be observed that ILSs at BA 11 are preceded and succeeded by activation of neurons in the same BA 11 but mostly at other cortical locations. Sequential cortical activation differs for groups G_1 and G_2, indicating that volunteers in these two groups enrolled different set of neurons to make decisions (see Figure 7.5) and use different temporal dynamics to support this reasoning.

In addition, these results are clear evidences for the distributed character of brain processing by showing how information is exchanged between neurons located at many different cortical areas.

By changing boundaries Area Subset on spreadsheet parameter, it is possible to study ILS sequence associated to other cortical areas other than BA 11.

7.8   LORETA Sources and Grand Average

It is possible to study the association between *Grand Averages* calculated for G_1 and G_2 and ILSs recruited for these groups when both amplitude and frequencies are considered. This may be done by superimposing the corresponding Amplitude or Band Frequency ILS temporal evolution and the corresponding *Grand Average* as in spreadsheet *Summary LORETA* (Figure 7.6).

Inspection of source temporal distribution in Figure 7.6 shows that, for both experimental groups, ILSs coded between 40 and 60 are active during most of the time either at the left or at the right hemisphere. Checking these codes in spreadsheet parameters reveals

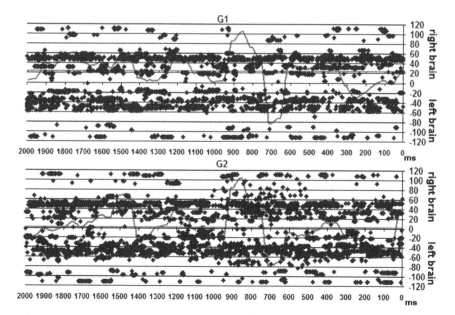

Figure 7.6   Superposition of temporal distribution upon the *Grand Average* (Figure 7.2). ILSs are coded as shown in spreadsheet *Parameters* labeled negative for locations at the left hemisphere and positive for the right hemisphere.

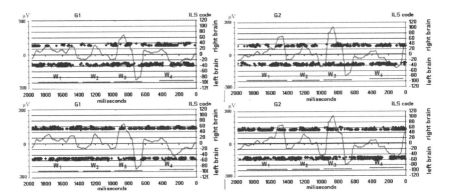

Figure 7.7 ILS temporal distribution for hubs in BA 10 and 11 (above) and BA 18 and 19 (below).

that these sources are located at BA 18 and 19. ILSs coded between 30 and 40 that are sources located at BA 10 and 11 are also frequently activated. Temporal distribution of sources coded between 80 and 120 are sparser than those discussed above. These results indicate that neurons at BA 18 or 19 and BA 10 or 11 operate as hubs in the nets supporting financial reasoning, because ILSs located at these sites are activated very frequently (see Figure 7.7). These networks are free-scale nets (see Section 3.5) that contain few nodes that are highly connected to other nodes. This structure, as discussed before, increases message spreading in the network at a low connectivity cost.

Now, if *subset* 1 is defined by the boundaries 60 and 113 and *subsets* 2 and 3 are set empty, the obtained results are those in Figure 7.8. Spatial ILS distribution shows that activated neurons are distributed over frontal, temporal and parietal cortices. Temporal ILS distribution shows that activated neurons seem to vary when the different EEG components (see Figure 7.2) are considered.

To further explore these differences, area subset 1 boundaries were restricted to 60 and 95 and the time window to those corresponding to components W_2 and W_3 by setting the time window flag to 1 and setting the values in cells B21 and B22 to 1. Figure 7.9 shows a striking difference in brain activity between the two groups at selected areas and time window. It may be observed that activity at temporal and parietal cortices predominates when G_2 is compared to G_1.

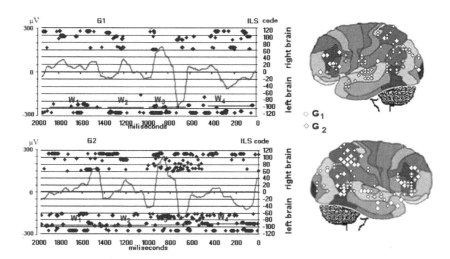

Figure 7.8 Temporal and spatial ILS distribution in the case of area codes 60–113.

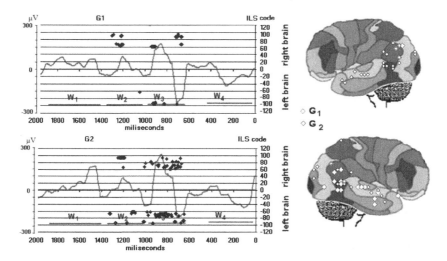

Figure 7.9 Temporal and spatial ILS distribution restrict to time windows corresponding to W_2 and W_3 in the case of area codes 60–95.

In contrast, restricting *subset* 1 boundaries to 100 and 113 and the time window being kept the same (Figure 7.10) show that neurons at frontal seems more active at left hemisphere in the case of G_1

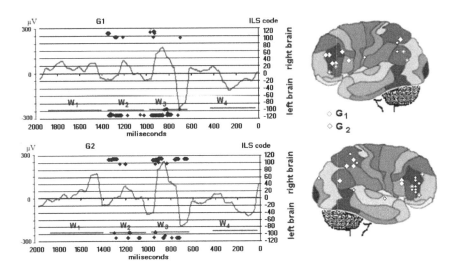

Figure 7.10 Temporal and spatial ILS distribution restrict to time windows corresponding to W_2 and W_3 in the case of area codes 100–113.

and at right hemisphere in G_2 case. In addition, activity at the right parietal cortex predominates in G_1 compared to G_2.

All these results strengthen the hypothesis that each experimental group uses a different type of reasoning to trade using the simulated game that is supported by different cortical activities. An important difference is related to pricing if W_3 is assumed to signal the moment volunteer is deciding about the price to be proposed for trading transaction.

7.9 $h(e_i)$ and Factor Analysis

Mappings in Figure 7.11 (and in spreadsheet *Factor Mappings*) color encode calculated mean $h(e_i)$ for each electrode and experimental groups G_1 and G_2 and they show that, for both groups, low values of $h(e_i)$ were obtained mostly for left temporal–parietal–occipital electrodes and the highest $h(e_i)$ values are associated with bilateral frontal electrodes. The G_1–G_2 mapping encodes the entropy differences between the two groups that are statistically significant and shows that entropy calculated for G_1 is larger than that calculated

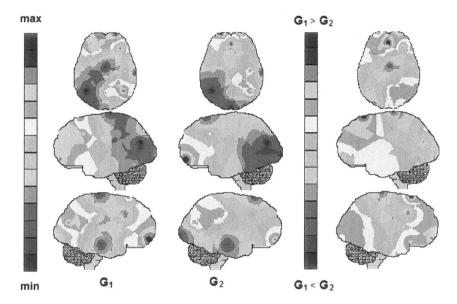

Figure 7.11 $h(e_i)$ mappings for experimental groups G_1 and G_2 and for the difference G_1–G_2. $h(e_i)$ and $h(e_i)$ differences were normalized and encoded according to the inserted scales.

for G_2 for bilateral frontal electrodes and right temporal–parietal electrodes. The reverse is true for the central electrode and the right parietal and occipital electrodes.

Mappings in Figure 7.12 (and in spreadsheet *Summary FA&LDA*) encode the results of Factor analysis (FA) carried out to study $h(e_i)$ covariation. Tables with these results are found in the yellow areas of spreadsheet *Factor Mappings*. Three different factors (labeled P_1, P_2 and P_3) with eigenvalues >1 explain 75 and 68% of $h(e_i)$ covariation in groups G_1 and G_2, respectively. Loadings of the 20 electrodes in these factors are clearly different for both experimental groups. Pattern (or factor) P_1 is mostly bilateral and frontal in G_1 case, and mostly bilateral and central in G_2 case. Pattern (or factor) P_2 is mostly composed by electrodes PZ, OZ and O2 in G_1 case, and by the electrodes F3, PZ, P_4, T6 and O1 in G_2 case. Finally, the pattern P_3 discloses associations between $h(e_i)$ calculated for electrodes F7, T3, T4, T5, C4 and P_4 in G_1 case and that calculated for electrodes FZ, T3, T5, P_3, OZ and O2 in G_2 case.

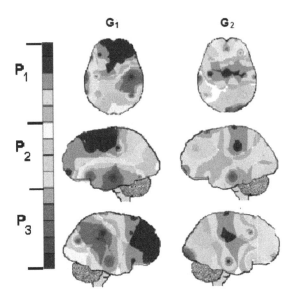

Figure 7.12 Factor mappings for experimental groups G_1 and G_2. Loading factors were normalized and encoded according to the inserted scale.

These results clearly show that reasoning about trading has very different dynamics in each experimental group. In the previous sections, it was shown that trading decision was supported by different sets of neurons widely distributed over the cortex, and now FA shows that dynamics of cortical activity differs for both G_1 and G_2, too.

7.10 Logistic Regression and Linear Discriminant Analysis

Logistic regression mapping in Figure 7.13 (and in spreadsheet *Summary FA&LDA*) correlating $h(e_i)$ and experimental group shows that high $h(e_i)$ values calculated for electrodes FP2, FZ, F3, T4, T5, T6, P_4, PZ and OZ predominated in G_1 volunteers, whereas high $h(e_i)$ values predominated in G_2 individuals for electrodes FP1, F4, CZ, P_3 and O1. These results are in accordance with $h(e_i)$ differences calculated between G_1 and G_2 shown in Figure 7.11.

Linear discriminant analysis (LDA) mappings in Figure 7.13 (and in spreadsheet *Summary FA&LDA*) show the statistical transition between G_1 and G_2 FA patterns. These intermediate patterns may represent cerebral dynamics of those individuals that used different

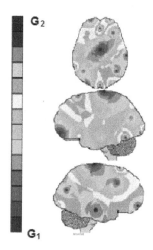

Figure 7.13 Logistic regression using the binary variable P that assumes value 0 for G_1 individuals and value 1 for G_2 volunteers. Angular coefficients were normalized in the interval $[-1, 1]$ (for G_1 and G_2) and encoded according to the inserted bar.

reasoning to support trading decisions about the different stocks, oscillating between reasoning characterized by FA for G_1 to that characterized for G_2.

LDA results show that G_1 trading brain activity is mostly characterized by values of $v(e_i, t)$ recorded by electrodes FP1, F4, CZ and C4 as shown by the first LDA mapping, whereas G_2 trading brain activity is mostly characterized by values of $v(e_i, t)$ recorded by electrodes FP2, F7, F3, FZ, F8, T6, P_4 and PZ as shown by the last (9) LDA mapping.

7.11 Associating LORETA Sources to FA and LDA Mappings

It is possible to explore the possible correlations between ILS and FA patterns. Because $v(e_i, t)$ recorded by electrode e_i is dependent on the distance from the electrical sources to the recording electrodes, and FA patterns are defined by electrode loading factors, it is highly probable that sources nearest to the electrodes specifying a given FA pattern are the main determinants of $h(e_i)$ covariation associated

A Practical Guide to Brain Data Analysis

Table 7.1 Suggested area selection to study LORETA and FA correlation.

Area selection	Group G_1		Group G_2	
	Lower	Upper	Lower	Upper
Pattern P_1				
Subset 1	100	113	100	111
Subset 2	0	40	65	66
Subset 3			0	22
Pattern P_2				
Subset 1	60	105	96	113
Subset 2	16	21	65	68
Subset 3	0	10	0	21
Pattern P_3				
Subset 1	60	64	110	113
Subset 2	40	55	50	55
Subset 3			30	33

with this pattern. This may be investigated by changing areas subset boundaries in *Parameters* checking resulting in *Summary & LDA* spreadsheet (see Table 7.1).

Mappings shown in Figure 7.14 were generated by setting subset boundaries assumed to correspond to areas whose activity would generate the distinct FA patterns identified for each experimental group. For instance, setting boundaries of *subset* 1 to 100 and 111 and of *subset* 2 to 0 and 40 select ILSs associated with pattern P_1 in G_1 (see Table 7.1). These ILSs may be identified in ILS frequency graph in *Summary LORETA*. In the same way, setting boundaries of *subset* 1 to 100 and 111, of *subset* 2 to 65 and 66 and of *subset* 2 to 0 and 22 select ILSs associated with pattern P_1 in G_2 and inspecting the same spreadsheet to identify ILSs generating this FA pattern. Table 7.1 displays area subset boundaries for all patterns and experimental groups.

You may try subset boundaries other than those in Table 7.1 to check whether you agree or disagree with results shown in

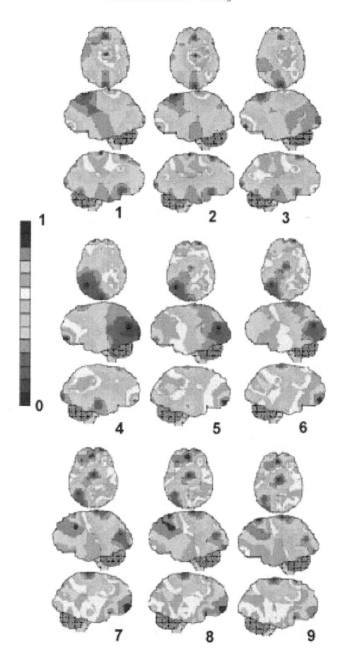

Figure 7.14 Correlating ILS spatial location and FA patterns for G_1 and G_2 according to area subsets defined in Table 7.1.

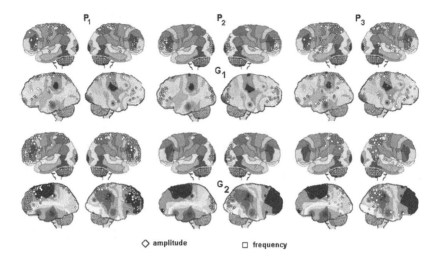

Figure 7.15 LDA loading factors were normalized and encoded according to the inserted bar.

Figure 7.14. Perhaps, a careful inspection of mappings in this figure may reveal some discrepancies of selected ILSs and FA patterns at right and left hemispheres.

Handling area subset boundaries allows you to identify, in spreadsheet *Summary FA&LDA*, those ILSs associated to ILSs associated to G_1–G_2 entropy differences shown in Figure 7.11; to logistic regression mapping in Figure 7.13 and LDA mappings displayed in Figure 7.15.

Results from all these analyses confirm the hypothesis that G_1 group predominantly relied on prospective reasoning because they learned how to play the game in a trendy market, whereas G_2 people predominantly relied on a retrospective reasoning because they started learning on a volatile market.

7.12   Multilinear Regression Analysis

Logistic regression analysis shows that gender correlates with $h(e_i)$ with R^2 equal to 36% (spreadsheet *Logistic Regression*). High $h(e_i)$ values at Fp2, F7, T3, T5 and CZ are characteristics of males, whereas high $h(e_i)$ values at F4, C4, PZ and CZ are found in female case (Figure 7.16). These results show that men and women seem

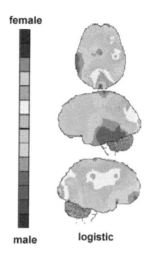

Figure 7.16 Gender logistic regression analysis. Angular coefficients were normalized in the interval $[-1, 1]$ (for male and female) and encoded according to the inserted bar.

to use different reasoning to support their financial decision-making (Rocha *et al.*, 2015).

Manipulation of control parameters at *Parameters* spreadsheet allows identifying ILSs that are associated with these logistic regression results. ILSs located mostly at the left BA 5, 6, 21, 37, 38, 39 and 40 predominated in males, whereas those located at mostly at BA 18 and 19 are mostly characteristics of the female reasoning. In addition, analysis of ILS frequency (*Summary LORE TA* spreadsheet) shows that these differences are more important for G_2 and G_1 when male and female predominant areas are compared.

Multilinear regression analysis may be used to study the correlation between financial variables and $h(e_i)$ as shown in Figure 7.17 (and *Summary Regression* spreadsheet). This analysis uses *gender* as dummy variable (male $= 0$ and female $= 1$) and $h(e_i)$ and *gender*h(e$_i$)* as independent variables. In these regressions, electrodes having positive betas are those for which high $h(e_i)$ is associated with perception of high-value portfolio or cash, whereas electrodes having negative betas are those for which high $h(e_i)$ is associated with perception of low-value portfolio or cash.

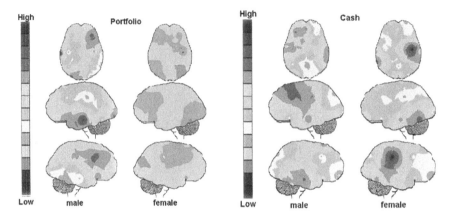

Figure 7.17 Multilinear regression analysis mappings as calculated in *MLR-Portfolio* and *MLR-Cash* spreadsheets angular coefficients were normalized in the interval $[-1, 1]$ (for low and high) and encoded according to the inserted bar.

Inspection of Figure 7.17 shows that men and women differ on these perceptions because the corresponding regression mappings are statically different as can be checked in *MRL-Portfolio* and *MRL-Cash* spreadsheets. In addition, it seems that brain activity on portfolio value and cash are reversed, with values of $h(e_i)$ associated with perception of high-valued portfolio being associated with perception of low cash and vice versa. This is easily understandable from the complementary role between portfolio value and cash. It is necessary to sell stocks to make cash and to buy stocks to increase investment.

If you have other questions about relationship between portfolio value or cash and brain activity or other hypotheses about financial decision-making, you may change control parameters in *Parameters* spreadsheet to check them.

7.13   Final Comments

A large number of different techniques for EEG analysis were employed in this chapter in an attempt to understand neural dynamics of financial decision-making. This approach clearly shows that decision-making recruits different neural circuits that are in charge of specific and distinct computations to solve defined subtasks such as value, benefit, risk analyses, stock selection, price estimation, etc. Different people recruit distinct neural circuits and combine them to support different reasoning modes that they judge to be more profitable for themselves. It is shown that the type of market people start to (learn to) trade is influential on selected reasoning strategies and that gender is also relevant for this choice.

Above all, discussions in the chapter clearly show that EEG technology has many advantages over other available techniques for brain activity recording, mostly because it provides an adequate time resolution for investigating this activity and, with modern statistical analyses, it allows for a suitable spatial location of the activated set of neurons and, more importantly, to study the dynamics of these activations.

References

Rocha, A.F., Massad, E., Pereira Jr., A. (2004). *The Brain: From Fuzzy Arithmetic to Quantum Computing.* Springer, Heidelberg, Germany.

Rocha, F.T., Rocha, A.F., Massad, E., Menezes, R. (2005). Brain mappings of the arithmetic processing in children and adults. *Cognitive Brain Research*, 22, 359–372.

Rocha, A.F., Vieito, E.J.P., Massad, E., Rocha, F.T., Lima, R.I. (2015). Electroencephalography activity associated to investment decisions: Gender differences. *Journal of Behavioral and Brain Science*, 5, 203–211. http://dx.doi.org/10.4236/jbbs.2015.56021.

Vieito, J., Rocha, A.F., Rocha, F.T. (2015). Brain activity of the investor's stock market financial decision. *Journal of Behavioral Finance*, 16, 1–11. doi: 10.1080/15427560.2015.1064931.

Chapter 8

Moral Dilemma Judgment

The purpose of this chapter is to discuss how neurosciences may contribute to the understanding of moral by studying Electroencephalogram (EEG) activity associated with moral dilemma judgment.

Greene *et al.* (2001) were among the first to use functional magnetic resonance imaging (fMRI) to study moral dilemma judgment. In two other papers (Greene *et al.*, 2004; Shenhav and Greene, 2010), they explore the cerebral areas involved in judgment of *personal* (PD) and *impersonal* (ID) like the trolley dilemma (as ID example) and the foot bridge dilemma (as PD example):

The trolley dilemma: (F) A runaway trolley is headed for five people who will be killed if it proceeds on its present course. (A) The only way to save them is to hit a switch that will turn the trolley onto an alternate set of tracks where it will kill one person instead of five. (D) Is it appropriate to switch the tracks?

The foot bridge dilemma: (F) Similar to the trolley dilemma, the trolley is on a path that will kill five people. (A) The five people could be saved if you push a stranger in front of the trolley; however, the stranger would be killed. (D) Is it appropriate to push the stranger?

Such dilemmas have the following structure:

— proposition F describes a situation that implies a social loss (dead) of a given value (five people);
— proposition A describes an action to avoid the social loss but at a personal risk of a given intensity (hitting a switch or pushing a stranger) and

— a question (D) asks the individual to decide whether A is appropriate in the context introduced by F.

Although the two dilemmas have the same logical structure, judgments about these two dilemmas are totally different because they imply similar benefit (avoid a given social loss) but at two different personal risks: hitting a switch = low risk or pushing a stranger = higher risk. Decision about saving 5 at the cost of killing 1 is taken by 50% of individuals for ID dilemma and only 30% of them for PD judgment, showing that the amount of personal risk is influential upon dilemma judgment (Rocha *et al.*, 2013a,b, 2014).

These results are in accordance with the neuroeconomic decision-making model proposed by Rocha *et al.* (2008). These authors proposed that, contrary to the general belief, cognition and emotion play complementary roles in any kind of decision-making because decision has to be guided by benefit versus risk analysis. As matter of fact, only recently Shenhav and Greene (2010) used regression analysis to correlate activity in previously chosen regions of interest and regressors like intended moral value (Shenhav and Greene, 2010) to study the dependence of dilemma judgment upon the expected benefit but not risk. This is in contrast with the concept of *utility* of an action as defined by Bentham (1789) who was among the first to propose the *theory of utilitarianism*. According to him, utility is dependent on both *pleasure* (benefit) and *pain* (risk) as estimated by the individual or the community.

Here, data from Rocha *et al.* (2013a) in EEG book *EEG_ Dilemma.xls* available at http://www.eina.com.br/software/ is used to discuss that moral dilemma judgment is supported by neuroeconomic reasoning that takes into account estimated personal and social benefits and risks as proposed by Rocha *et al.* (2013b).

8.1   Experimental Design

Greene *et al.* (2004) presented each dilemma as a text through a series of three screens, the first two describing F and A, and the last posing the question D. Subjects read at their own pace, pressing a button to advance from the first to the second screen and from the second to the third screen. However, because of the well-known fMRI time resolution constraints, Greene *et al.* (2004) used a floating window of eight images surrounding the time of response (four prior to, one during and three following), when individuals pressed one of the two buttons ("appropriate" or "inappropriate") according to their dilemma judgment. They included three post-response images in order to allow for the lag in BOLD response (typically peaking the after 3–5 s of eliciting a neural response). Therefore, their fMRI analysis involved a global time widow of 16 s long that did not discriminate among the distinct cerebral processing required by F, A and D phases of dilemma judgment. In all their papers (Greene *et al.*, 2001, 2004; Shenhav and Greene, 2010), the authors described around 30 different cortical areas as involved in dilemma judgment.

Rocha *et al.* (2013a) recorded EEG activity (Figure 8.1) while volunteers were making judgments about the same dilemma studied by Greene *et al.* (2001, 2004). Individuals were allowed free time to

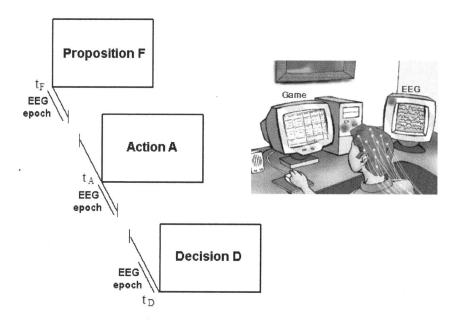

Figure 8.1 Experimental protocol to study dilemma judgment.

read propositions F and A as well as to make a decision D. They were requested to press OK button to move from F to A at instant t_F and from A to D at instant t_A. Finally, they have to press *Appropriate* or *Inappropriate* button to make the judgment at instant t_D. The most important difference between the present EEG study and previous fMRI investigations is that three EEG epochs of 2 s prior to button pressing were selected for studying the brain activity associated with dilemma understanding and judgment.

8.2   The Experimental Setting

Two laptops were used to run the experiment (Figure 8.1). One of them is in charge of EEG data acquisition and the other to display F, A and D screens and save t_F, t_A and t_D values as well as judgment (*Appropriate* = 1 and *Inappropriate* = 0). The clocks of both computers are synchronized. Because the two laptop clocks were synchronized, it was possible to localize, later, in the EEG file, the moments when volunteer made decisions.

Here, EEG epochs of 2 s were selected before each time OK button was pressed (Figure 8.1), each one corresponding to understanding (F and A) and judgment (D) decisions about 30 dilemmas. Experimental group was composed by 11 females and 12 males, therefore 1,070 EEG epochs were saved on *txt* files, each file containing 20 lines (one for each electrode) with 512 $v(e_i, t)$ measurements corresponding to the EEG sampled at the rate of 256 Hz during the 2 s prior to each decision button pressing.

8.3   EEG Components Identified in Grand Average

Four EEG components (W_1–W_4) were identified (Figure 8.2) in EEG Grand Average (Section 5.3.1) from $-1,900$ to $-1,350$, $-1,350$ to $-1,000$, -100 to -650 and -600 to 0 ms, for experimental phases F, A and D. Components W_2 and W_3 are mostly characterized by positive waves in contrast to components W_3 and W_4 that are mostly characterized by negative waves. Components W1 and W4 may be decomposed, respectively, into subcomponents W_{1a} ($-1,900$ to $-1,700$) and

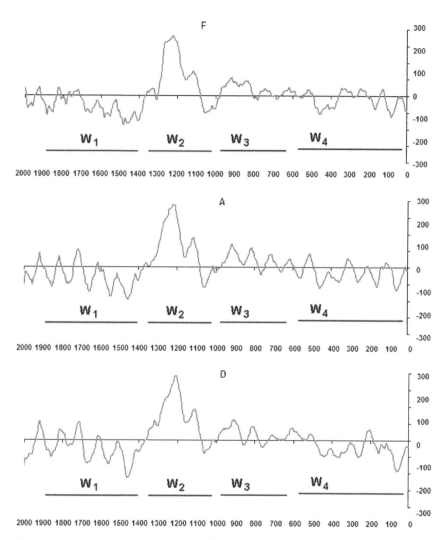

Figure 8.2 Grand averages and EEG waves as seen in spreadsheet *EEG components* and calculated for phases F, A and D from data on spreadsheets *Averaged EEG*.

W_{1b} (−1,700 to −1,350), and subcomponents W_{4a} (from −600 to −300) and W_{4b} (−300 to 0). Z-score analysis shows that more than 95% of the sampled EEG moments are significant at a threshold level of 2 (see Percentage of significant moments in *EEG components*).

A fivefold increase in this threshold results in reduction of around 25% of these significant moments, stressing that the results are robust.

Dilemma judgment requires simulating conditions described by propositions F and A for evaluation of possible social risk and benefit in F and possible personal risk and benefit in A. Simulations are required because, in general, dilemmas are highly hypothetical (as in the Trolley examples). The results of benefit and risk evaluations are used to calculate adequateness of action proposed in A (Rocha *et al.*, 2013b), which means to judge it as appropriate or too risky (or inappropriate). All these pieces of information are held in memory and compared during phase D to determine the type of judgment to be made.

In this context, it is proposed here that component W_1 signals ending of simulation period in F and A; W_2 and W_3 correlate with risk and benefit analysis, respectively, and W_4 corresponds to activity in calculating action adequateness. These calculations are carried out for actions described during phases F and A. Decision-making is dependent on the balance between adequateness of actions in F and D. In this way, it is proposed here that, during phase D, component W_1 signals brain activity associated with this comparison; W_2 and W_3 correlate with final checking of risk and benefit analysis and W_4 corresponds to activity in selecting action based on calculated action adequateness.

Linear regression analysis of Grand Averages calculated for F, A and D shows that the activity on phase D is more correlated to that on A than that on F (see graphic in spreadsheet *EEG components*), indicating that perhaps decision is much more related with analysis of personal risk and benefit carried out at phase A than on analysis of social risk and benefit carried out at phase F.

8.4 Activated Cortical Areas

Spreadsheet *Histograms* show the frequencies of location of identified LORETA source (ILS) over the different cortical areas. Inspection of these data shows that activity at BA 10, 11, 18, 19, 21, 22 and 46 predominated during F and A in comparison to D. These differences

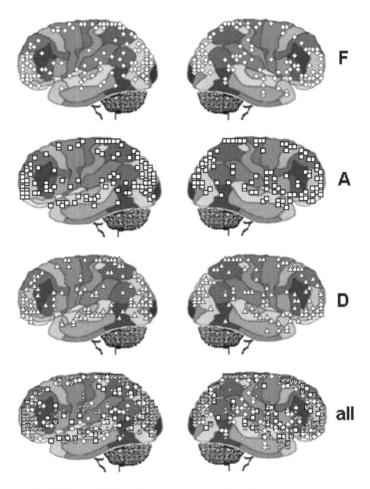

Figure 8.3 ILS spatial location as seen in *Amplitude source mappings* and *Summary LORETA* spreadsheets. F = proposition; A = action; D = decision.

are confirmed by the mappings showing ILS spatial location in Figure 8.3 that in addition reveal that many sources have the same XYZ coordinates but location of many other sources are phase-specific.

Mappings in Figure 8.4 (and spreadsheet *Summary LORETA*) show that the most important differences on ILS location when the different experimental phases were compared are found on BA 38, 39, 40, 41, 42, 43, 44 and 45. Locations at BA 10, 11, 18 and 19 tend to be similar for all experimental phases.

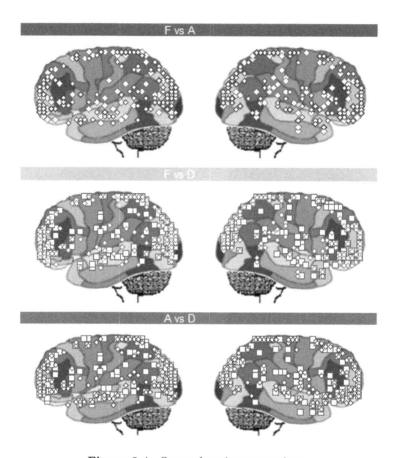

Figure 8.4 Source location comparison.

These results show that different brain activities are associated with risk and benefit analysis in social (phase F) and personal (phase A) contexts providing experimental support for the proposition made by Rocha *et al.* (2009) that these analyses are performed by different neural circuits called personal (PDS) and interpersonal (IDS) decision spaces, and used for calculating intentions to cooperate (to be altruist) or compete (to be selfish). Moral rules are thought, in general, to promote altruism or at least to disfavor endemic selfishness. PDS and IDS are circuits that compose what may be called the social brain as a collection of neural circuits to handle other intentions, cooperative actions, fair individual and collective decisions, etc. (Adolphs, 2009; Fehr and Gächte, 2002; Frith and Frith, 2007; Güroğlu *et al.*, 2010a,b; Rocha *et al.*, 2009).

8.5   EEG Band Frequencies

Comparison of band frequency ILS in spreadsheet *Histograms* shows that different ILS sets are associated to phases F, A and D. ILS spatial location also differed for the different phases of dilemma understanding and judgment (Figure 8.5). Differences in spatial location are observed for all band frequencies and are larger for the left hemisphere in comparison to the right brain. In addition, location of band frequency ILSs calculated for phase D differed from spatial location

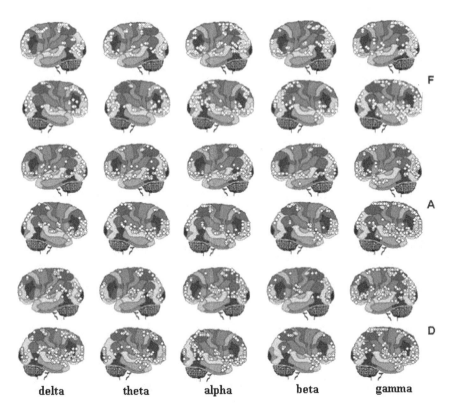

delta   theta   alpha   beta   gamma

Figure 8.5   Locations of all ILSs for the different band frequency and experimental phases F, A and D.

calculated for F and A mostly at BA 40, 41, 42 and 43 in the left hemisphere. Sources at these locations are more frequent and widespread during D than during the other phases and these differences are true for all band frequencies.

Another clear difference on source location concerns areas BA 1, 2, 3, 5 and 7 that predominate during F for all band frequencies at the left hemisphere but not for the right brain. Sources at BA 38 are observed for most of the band frequencies and mostly at the right brain during A and D. Finally, a larger number of ILS is observed at right BA 10 and 11 than at the left brain.

Temporal distribution of ILSs located at BA 10 and 11 as well as at BA 18 and 19 is high and almost uniform, showing that the neurons located at these areas act as hubs in the neural network recruited for moral dilemma judgment, as predicted if these networks are scale-free networks (Rocha *et al.*, 2010).

You may check for other differences handling control parameters in spreadsheet *Parameters*. Change the significance threshold to check for data robustness.

8.6   Cortical Activation

Figure 8.6 shows mappings that combined both amplitude and band frequency sources. Inspection of data in this figure (see the corresponding color mappings in spreadsheet *Summary LORETA*) shows that amplitude and band frequency sources are mostly located at the same spatial location, confirming the hypothesis that band frequency analysis disclosed how incoming information is retained in different time windows (frequencies) for further processing. However, some band frequency sources are located at slightly different cortical places in the same BA, showing that incoming information storage is a little more complex.

Mappings in Figure 8.6 show that brain activity during F, A and D is more alike in the right hemisphere than in the left brain. The differences in this case are identified mostly at the temporal and parietal lobes for all experimental phases. Check these differences by changing control parameters in the spreadsheet *Parameters*.

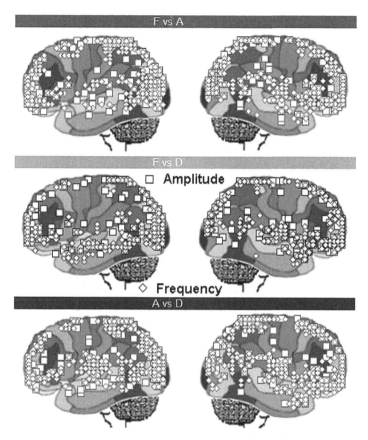

Figure 8.6 Locations of all ILSs for the different experimental phases F, A and D.

8.7 ILS Sequence

As discussed in Chapter 4, neurons located at BA 39–43 and BA 47 are involved in calculations of personal and third person intention of acting (see Figures 4.9 and 4.10). These areas are selected for analysis by setting boundaries of *subset* 1 to 90 and 105. Figure 8.7 (mappings IA) shows the spatial distribution of activation of these areas during phases F, A and D. Inspection of IA mappings shows that activation of these areas predominates at the right hemisphere and varies according to the dilemma judging phase. These areas are particularly active during phase D.

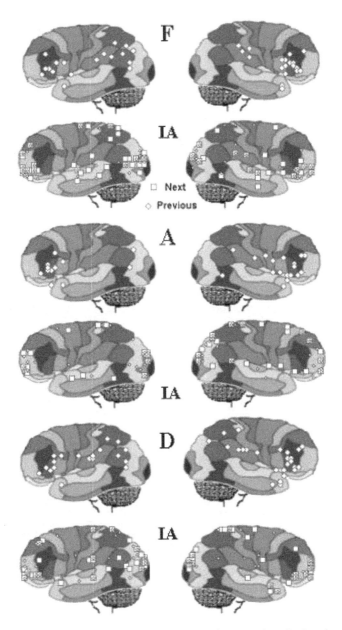

Figure 8.7 Locations of areas activated prior (previous) and after (next) activation of BA 39–43 and BA 47 (IA) during the distinct experimental phases F, A and D.

Figure 8.7 also displays the spatial location of ILSs that were activated prior (previous) or after (next) areas involved in calculating action intention. It can be easily observed that neurons located mostly at BA 4, 7, 9, 10, 11, 18 and 19 are either previously or subsequently activated after activation at BA 39–43 and BA 47 is identified. Around 30% of previous or next activated cortical areas are located at BA 10 and 11, showing that estimation of benefit and risk provides key information for calculation of action intention.

8.8 Low Resolution Tomography (LORETA) Sources and Grand Average

It is possible to study the association between *Grand Averages* and ILS obtained for the different experimental phases when both amplitude and frequencies are considered. This may be done by superimposing the corresponding amplitude or band frequency ILS temporal evolution and the corresponding *Grand Average* as in spreadsheet *Summary LORETA* (Figure 8.8). Results confirm the distributed character of brain activity associated with moral dilemma judgment (Rocha *et al.*, 2013a,b).

ILS temporal distribution during F has low correlation coefficients when compared to A ($R = 0.18$) or D ($R = 0.23$). In contrast, correlation coefficient is 0.88 for ILS temporal distribution during A and D. This may be interpreted by assuming that brain activity during D is much more correlated with that recorded during A than to that recorded during F. If this is true, then the hypothesis that computations during A are much more influential than those calculations performed during F upon brain activity supporting decision-making during D gains plausibility.

ILS temporal distribution shows that a large number of sources are activated during each phase of dilemma analysis, and picture displayed in Figure 8.8 is very complex and seems unintelligible. However, a careful inspection of the figure shows that ILSs coded between 30–40 and 50–60 are active most of the time, in contrast, for example, to ILSs coded from 80 to 100. ILSs coded from 100 to 113 are activated more frequently at the right hemisphere in contrast to left brain.

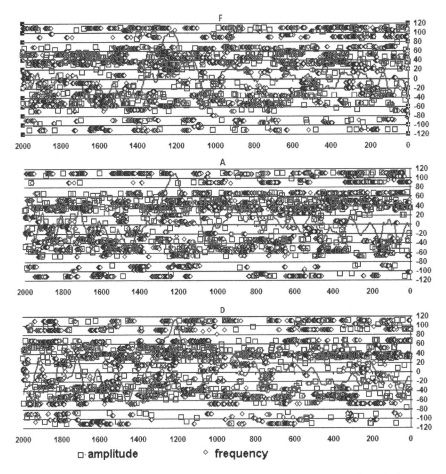

Figure 8.8 Superposition of temporal distribution upon the *Grand Average* (Figure 8.2).

Rocha *et al.* (2010) proposed that reasoning recruits scale-free neural networks are networks having nodes that are heavily connected to other nodes in the net and whose function is to reduce cost of spreading information throughout the network. Areas BA 10 and 11 (coded from 30 to 40) and BA 18 and 19 (coded from 50 to 60) seem to play the role of hubs in the neural network recruited for dilemma judgment, because they are continuously activated during the entire analyzed EEG epoch. Neurons at other cortical areas that are not continuously activated are supposed to enroll in solving specific subtasks for dilemma judgment. For example, neurons at temporal and parietal cortices are proposed to be involved in calculating action adequateness and others intention.

Temporal distribution of ILS location at BA 21, 22, 39, 40, 42 and 47 that are involved in intention of acting (see Sections 4.8 and 4.9) was studied by controlling time window in *Parameters* and results are shown in Figure 8.9. It seems that band frequency ILSs seem to be much more active during W_2 and W_3 periods in phase D compared to that in phases F and A. These differences are more evident for activity in the right brain during W_2 and in the left brain during W_3. In addition, ILS distribution seems to be more alike for A, F and D during W_1 and W_4 periods. These results may support the hypothesis proposed in Section 8.3 that during phase D, component W_1 signals brain activity associated with action adequateness comparison; W_2 and W_3 correlate with final checking of risk and benefit analysis and W_4 corresponds to activity in selecting action based on calculated action adequateness.

8.9 $h(e_i)$ and Factor Analysis

Mappings in Figure 8.10 (and in spreadsheet *Summary FA*) encode calculated mean $h(e_i)$ for each electrode and experimental phases F, A and D. Factor analysis (FA) identified two patterns of covariation during F and A and three patterns during D. Pattern P_1 during F and A is mostly composed by all frontal and central electrodes plus T3, while P_2 is composed by all parietal and occipital electrodes plus T5, T4 and T6. Pattern P_1 during D is composed by all frontal electrodes, while pattern P_2 is composed by T4, T5, O1, O2 and OZ. Pattern P_3 is distinctive for D and is composed by all central and parietal electrodes plus P3.

Contribution of each ILS to $v(e_i, t)$ recorded by each electrode e_i is dependent on the distance between the source and the recording electrode. Because of this, sources located nearest to the electrodes having high loading in each pattern P_i may be considered as contributing to the $h(e_i)$ covariation detected by each of these factors.

130   *A Practical Guide to Brain Data Analysis*

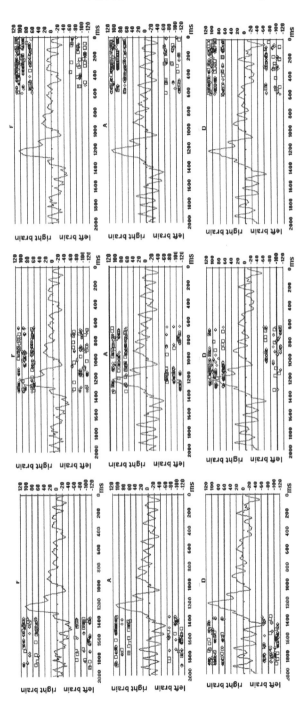

Figure 8.9 Temporal evolution of ILSs located at BA 21, 22, 39, 40, 42 and 47 that are involved in intention of acting.

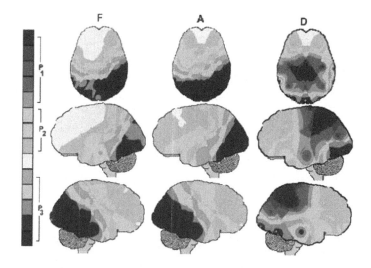

Figure 8.10 $h(e_i)$ mappings for experimental phases F, D and A.

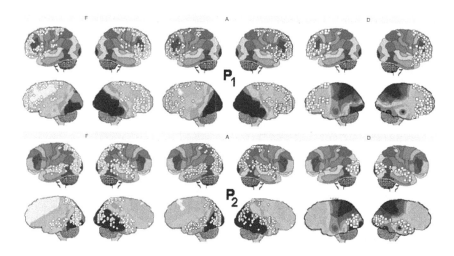

Figure 8.11 ILSs associated with patterns P_1 and P_2.

Mappings in Figures 8.11 and 8.12 show that the ILSs nearest to electrodes loading in P_1 and P_2 for the experimental phases F, A and D. Area subset boundaries in Table 8.1 were used to study correlation between ILS spatial distribution and FA pattern. By selecting area,

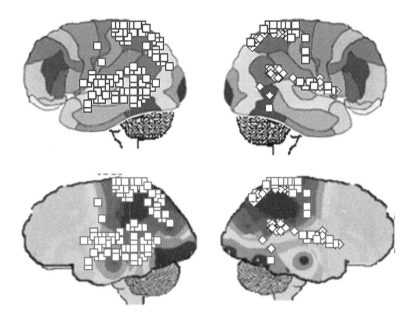

Figure 8.12 ILSs associated with patterns P_3.

Table 8.1 Use area subset boundaries.

Cortical area	Lower ILS code	Upper ILS code
Pattern P_1		
Subset 1	85	100
Subset 2	60	70
Subset 3	16	21
Pattern P_2		
Subset 1	100	113
Subset 2	22	40
Subset 3	10	16
Pattern P_3		
Subset 1	60	80
Subset 2	0	21
Subset 3		

these subset boundaries in spreadsheet *Parameters*, it is possible to recreate these mappings in spreadsheet *Summary FA*.

Considering phases F and A, pattern P_2 seems to be determined by covariation of activity in neurons located at BA 6, 8, 9, 10, 11, 38, 40 44, 45, 46 and 47, whereas pattern P_1 seems to be related with activity in BA 7, 18, 19, 21, 22, 37, 41 and 42. Because actions proposed by proposition F and A are highly hypothetical, reasoning about them has to be supported by simulating the described events. In this context, it may be proposed here that pattern P_2 disclose cortical activity involved in planning and controlling such simulations as well as evaluating action value, risk and benefit. In the same line of reasoning, it may be proposed that activity disclosed by pattern P_1 results from caring out these simulations.

Pattern P_3 identified only during D phase is mostly associated to activity located at BA 1–7, BA 21, 22, 38, 39, 40 and 42 that, as discussed before, are proposed to be involved in calculating action adequateness and intention of acting taking into account both personal and social points of view. Also, it is interesting to observe that patterns P_2 and P_3 during D seem to be component of pattern P_2 calculated during F and A. It may be accepted that activity of neural circuits that correlated during F and A are, now, uncorrelated during D. More precisely, it seems that visual activity in BA 18 and 19 becomes independent from that at BA 7, 21, 22, 37 and 39 probably involved in calculating adequateness of action to dilemma solving. This makes sense if it is remembered that simulations during F and A required calculations of adequateness of possible actions imagined by activity of BA 18 and 18.

If you have doubts about the hypotheses being proposed here, you may changes control parameter at spreadsheet *Parameters* to support your questions.

8.10 Multilinear Regression Analysis

Logistic regression analysis shows that gender correlates with $h(e_i)$ with R^2 equal to 29% (spreadsheet *Logistic Regression*). High $h(e_i)$ values at F3, C3, F4 and P4 are characteristics of males, whereas

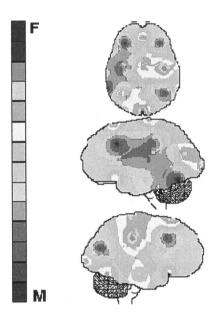

Figure 8.13 Gender logistic regression analysis.

high $h(e_i)$ values at FZ, CZ, PZ, OZ, C4, T6 and P3 are found in female cases (Figure 8.13 and spreadsheet *Summary Regression*). These results show that men and women seem to use different types of reasoning to make moral dilemma judgment.

Manipulation of control parameters in *Parameters* spreadsheet allows for identification of ILSs that are associated with these gender differences. Activity of neurons at BA 21, 22, 38, 39, 40, 44, 45 and 47, mostly at the left hemisphere, seems to be better associated with male than to female reasoning. In contrast, activity of neurons at BA 19, 20, 21 and 22, mostly at the right hemisphere, seems to be better associated with female than to male reasoning. Perhaps, these results may indicate that female reasons more taking a social perspective and male reasons more from a personal point of view. If you disagree, make your own analysis changing control parameters in *Parameters* spreadsheet.

Multilinear regression analysis was used to study the correlation between $h(e_i)$ and dilemma judgment (spreadsheet *MRL-Decision*) or response time (spreadsheet *Summary Regression*). Analysis in these spreadsheets uses *gender* as dummy variable (male $= 0$ and female $= 1$) and $h(e_i)$ and *gender*$*h(e_i)$ as independent variables. Resulting regression mappings are shown in Figure 8.14.

The most important electrodes in decision regression mappings are FP1, FP2, T5, T6 and F8 for both males and females and P3 for females. For both genders, high $h(e_i)$ values for electrodes F8 are associated to judging action proposed in A as appropriate, in contrast high $h(e_i)$ values for electrodes T4 are associated to judging action proposed in A as inappropriate. High $h(e_i)$ for electrodes FP1 and FP2 have opposite influence upon dilemma judgment for males and females. Finally, high $h(e_i)$ values for electrodes P3 are associated to females judging action proposed in A as appropriate.

Analysis of spatial ILS location associated with dilemma judgment shows that proposed action in A tends to be considered as appropriate when neurons at BA 10, 11, 21 and 22 are activated mostly at the left hemisphere and judged as inappropriate when these neurons are activated mostly at the right hemisphere.

For both genders high $h(e_i)$ values for electrodes CZ and PZ are associated with long response times, while high $h(e_i)$ values for electrode T5 and OZ are associated with short response times. $h(e_i)$ calculated for electrodes FP1 and C3 has opposite influence on how long individuals take to judgment when gender is taken into consideration. Finally, $h(e_i)$ is inversely correlated with response time in males.

Analysis of spatial ILS location shows that response time tends to be low when judgment is more influenced left cortical areas involved in analysis from the personal point of view and high when predominates activity at areas involved with value, benefit and risk analysis as well as with attention control. These later areas seem to be more important in the case of female reasoning, while the former were more influential on male reasoning.

8.11 Final Comments

Results described in this chapter based on EEG analysis may be compared to those published by Greene *et al.* (2001, 2004) and Shenhav

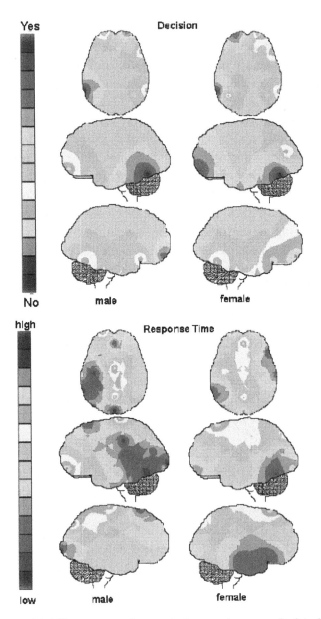

Figure 8.14 Multilinear regression analysis mappings as calculated in *MLR-Decision* and *MLR-Response time* spreadsheets.

and Greene (2010) using fMRI. This comparison is straightforward because the same dilemma was used by these authors and in the studies by Rocha *et al.* (2013a,b) and also available in *EEG_Dilemma* book.

This comparison is important because it clearly shows that available tools for EEG analysis allows analysis of neural processing supporting dilemma judgment more complex than that supported by fMRI studies. This stress the claim in this book that EEG is the tool of choice for studying brain activity associated with decision-making if focus of investigation is on cortical, but not subcortical structures.

References

Adolphs, R. (2009). The social brain: Neural basis of social knowledge. *Annual Review of Psychology*, 60, 693–716. doi:10.1146/annurev.psych. 60.110707.163514.

Bentham, J. (1789). Introduction to the principles of morals and legislation. In: Burns, J.H., Dinwiddy, J.R., Rosen, F., Schofield, T.P. (Eds.) *The Collected Works of Jeremy Bentham*. Athlone Press, London/Clarendon Press, Oxford.

Fehr, E., Gächte, S. (2002). Altruistic punishment in humans. *Nature*, 415, 137–140. doi:10.1038/415137a.

Frith, C., Frith, U. (2007). Social cognition in humans. *Current Biology*, 17, 315–320.

Greene, J.D., Sommerville, R.B., Nystrom, L.E., Darley, J.M., Cohen, J.D. (2001). An fMRI investigation of emotional engagement in moral judgment. *Science*, 293, 2105–2108.

Greene, J.D., Nystrom, L.E., Nystrom, A.D., Engel, A.D., Darley, J.M., Cohen, J.D. (2004). The neural bases of cognitive conflict and control in moral judgment. *Neuron*, 44, 389–400.

Güroğlu, B., van den Bos, W., Rombouts, S.A.R.B., Crone, E.A. (2010a). Unfair? It depends: Neural correlates of fairness in social context. *Social Cognitive and Affective Neuroscience*. doi: 10.1093/scan/nsq013.

Güroğlu, B., van den Bos, W., van Dijk, E., Rombouts, S.A.R.B., Crone, E.A. (2010b). Dissociable brain networks involved in development of fairness considerations: Understanding intentionality behind unfairness. *NeuroImage*, 2, 634–641.

Rocha, A.F., Burattini, M.N., Rocha, F.R., Massad, E. (2009). A neuroeconomic modeling of attention deficit and hyperactivity disorder. *Journal of Biological Systems*, 17, 597–621.

Rocha, A.F., Rocha, F.T., Massad, E. (2013a). Moral dilemma judgment revisited: A LORETA analysis. *Journal of Behavioral and Brain Science*. doi: 10.4236/jbbs.2013.38066.

Rocha, A.F., Rocha, F.T., Massad, E. (2013b). Moral dilemma judgment: A neuroeconomic approach. *Cognitive Social Science eJournal*, 5(60). http://papers.ssrn.com/abstract=2314771.

Rocha, A.F., Massad, E., Rocha, F.T., Burattini, M.N. (2014). Brain and law: an EEG study of how we decide or not to implement a law. *Journal of Behavioral and Brain Science*, 4, 559–578. http://dx.doi.org/10.4236/jbbs.2014.412054.

Shenhav, A., Greene, J.D. (2010). Moral judgments recruit domain-general valuation mechanisms to integrate representations of probability and magnitude. *Neuron*, 67, 667–677.

Chapter 9

Thinking about Firearm Control

From time to time, passionate debates arise about firearm commerce due to mass killing motivated by social or religious issues in many societies around the world. Ten years ago, Brazil held a referendum about firearm commerce prohibition.

Voting is mandatory in Brazil, and political campaign takes advantage of Radio/TV free propaganda 40 days before election. Two political alliances arouse in the Brazilian Congress to run the campaign for the Yes (favoring prohibition of firearm commerce) and No (against the prohibition of firearm commerce) voting. The media campaign stressed the benefits and costs of each decision, trying to oppose the benefits of one decision against the risks of the opposite one.

Rocha *et al.* (2010, 2014) recorded the electroencephalogram (EEG) activity of 32 individuals one week before the election day, while they declared their vote intention and provide information if six of most arguments used by media propaganda were trustful and would influence their vote.

Here, the results of these studies, described in the EEEG books *EEE_Voting* and *EEG_Marketing* available at http://www.eina.com. br/software/, are used to discuss how EEG may be used to study collective decision-making and how brain processes media propaganda.

9.1 Experimental Design

Thirty-two subjects, 16 female and 16 male adults (Table 9.1), had their EEG registered with 20 electrodes placed according to the 10/20 system; impedance < 10 kΩ; low band passing filter 50 Hz;

Table 9.1   Poll opinion questionnaire.

Select a response below that best describes your opinion about the ban on
  firearm commerce in Brazil.
You may provide a second response if you believe that your first response may
  change by election day:
I will certainly vote No,
I will probably vote No,
Certainly, I will not vote No,
I have not yet decided my vote,
I will certainly vote Yes,
I will probably vote Yes,
Certainly, I will not vote Yes.

Marketing
Here, you are asked to provide your opinion about some statements that have
  been made in free propaganda on the radio and TV.
Please select one of the following options that best describes your opinion about
  this statement:
(a) *I believe*   (b) *I do not believe*   (c) *I have no opinion*
Please select one of the following options to evaluate the influence of this
  statement on your vote on election day:
(a) *It will influence my vote*   (b) *It will not influence my vote*   (c) *I do not
  know*
1 or Y1: *A gun in the house may cause a fatal accident, killing innocent people,
  mainly children. You may prevent such events by banning firearm commerce.*
2 or N1: *People have the right to defend themselves from criminals. The proposal
  of banning firearm commerce hurts your personal rights.*
3 or Y2: *Having a gun facilitates murder in the case of a neighboring, family or
  traffic dispute. You may prevent such events by banning firearm commerce.*
4 or Y3: *The robbery of firearms from an honest citizen is the main source of
  guns for criminals. You may contribute to disarm criminals by banning
  firearm commerce.*
5 or N2: *To ban firearm commerce disarms honest citizens but not criminals.*
6 or N3: *To prohibit firearm commerce will not reduce criminal rates.*

---

sampling rate of 256 Hz and 10 bits resolution while declaring their
vote intention and answering question about media propaganda (see
Table 9.1).

Two networked personal computers were used (Figure 9.1), one
for the EEG recording and the other for presenting the questionnaire. The volunteers were allowed to take as much time as needed to
make any decision pressing the adequate decision button. The EEG

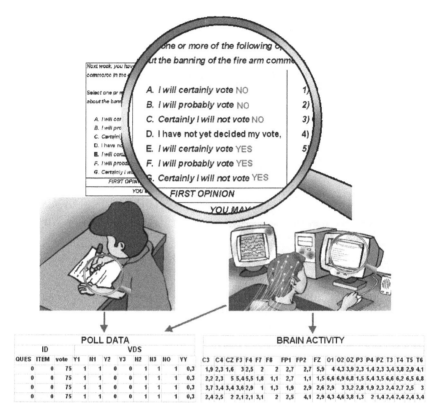

Figure 9.1 Experimental protocol brain activity associated with vote decision.

Table 9.2 Characteristics of the sampled population.

Age		Gender		Instruction		Income	
Mean	35	Female	0.42	Elementary school	0.17	Low	0.41
Max	63	Male	0.58	High school	0.30	Medium	0.44
Min	18			College	0.53	High	0.27

recorded during the 2 s preceding the decision button was used for analysis.

For control purpose, another group of 1,136 people living in the Great São Paulo area answered in writing the same poll opinion questionnaire in Table 9.1. Table 9.2 provides information about the studied population.

9.2   Brain Activity Associated with Vote Decision

This section of the chapter focuses on the analysis of the EEG epochs associated with vote decision using data from *EEG_vote.xls*.

Poll results (Rocha *et al.*, 2010) showed that, one week before election day, around 62% of interviewed people declared intention (of variable degree) to vote No and 30% of them declared intention (of variable degree) to vote No. Results in election day showed that 61% of voters decided to reject firearm commerce prohibition voting No and 28% of them supported prohibiting voting Yes. Interesting to remark is the fact that professional pollsters indicated even at the night before election day that intentions to vote Yes or No were equilibrated around 50%.

9.2.1   Averaged EEG

EEG epochs associated to each type of vote (No and Yes) were averaged (see Section 5.3.1) to be used for Low resolution tomography (LORETA) analysis and calculation of respective the grand averages (Figure 9.2 and spreadsheet *EEG components*).

Four EEG components (W_1–W_4) were identified in Grand Averages (see Section 5.3.1) from $-1,900$ to $-14,500$, $-1,400$ to $-1,000$, -950 to -500 and -400 to 0 ms (see yellow cells in time window section of *Parameter*). Components W_2 and W_3 are mostly characterized by positive waves in contrast to components W_3 and W_4 that are mostly characterized by negative waves. Z score analysis shows that more than 70% of the sampled EEG moments are significant at a threshold level of 2 (see percentage of significant moments in *EEG components*). A fivefold increase in this threshold results reduced significant moments to 20% of the 512 sample moments, showing that the results are robust.

Linear regression analysis of Grand Averages calculated for No and Yes vote shows that these responses tend to be uncorrelated because R^2 is around 0.06 (see *EEG components*).

Once the type of vote is decided, individuals have to calculate its adequacy and how much they are committed to their decisions. Here, it is proposed that component W_1 is associated with deciding about

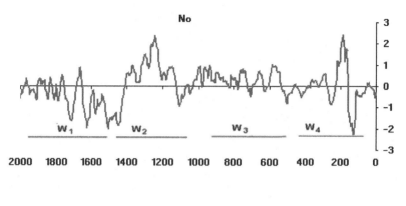

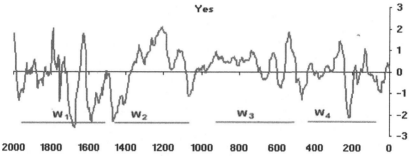

Figure 9.2 Grand Averages calculated for No and Yes votes and EEG components as seen in spreadsheet *EEG components*.

vote type, while components W_2 and W_3 are related to the calculations about vote. Perhaps, W_2 is associated with vote adequateness calculation and W_3 is related with vote intention (willingness) estimation (see Figure 2.2). Finally, component W_4 is assumed to reflect decision button pressing.

9.2.2 Activated cortical areas

Figure 9.3 (see also spreadsheets *Amplitude Sources frequency* and *Band Sources frequency*) shows the difference between frequencies of location for both amplitude and band identified LORETA sources (ILS) identified as first solution for EEG epochs for No and Yes votes according to the code listed in the spreadsheet *Parameters*. It can be seen that activity at BA 10 — Superior Frontal Gyrus, BA 11 — Middle and Superior Frontal Gyrus, BA 18 — Cuneus, BA 18 —

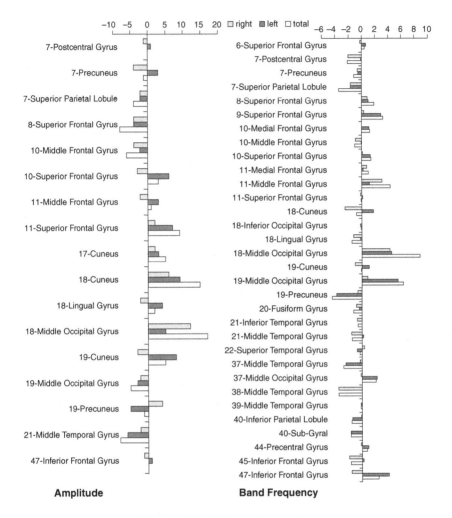

Figure 9.3   ILS spatial location.

Middle Occipital Gyrus and BA 19 — Cuneus predominate for No in comparison to Yes vote both in the case of Amplitude and Band ILSs. In contrast, activity at BA 7, 19 and 21 predominated for Yes in comparison to No vote for the same ILSs. Other frequency differences between are observed for other locations.

Figure 9.4 (see also spreadsheet *Summary LORETA*) shows that spatial location of ILSs associated with No vote decision is different

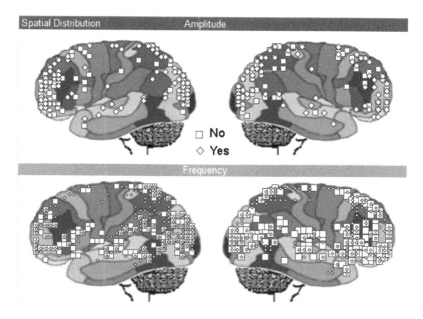

Figure 9.4 Amplitude and frequency ILS spatial location.

from that for Yes vote intention. These differences predominate at BA 7, 8, 9, 22, 39 to 44 and 46. It must be remarked that similar number of significant moments (number of time moments t when Z score for $v(e_i, t)$ is greater than the significance threshold in *Parameters*) are observed for the two types of vote. These differences may be explored by changing area subset boundaries and time window in *Parameters*. This may help you to train your skills as a neuroscientist.

9.2.3 ILS sequence

Spreadsheets *Connectivity* display the spatial location of the Brodmann areas that are identified by LORETA as activated previously and after the actual ILSs specified in spreadsheet *Parameters*.

Inspection of ILS frequency in spreadsheet *Amplitude Sources frequencies* that sources located at BA 10 (codes 30–33), BA 11 — Superior Frontal Gyrus (code 39), BA 18 — Cuneus (code 47) and BA 18 — Middle Occipital Gyrus (code 52) predominates for both types

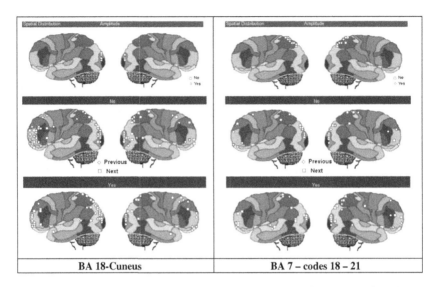

| BA 18-Cuneus | BA 7 – codes 18 – 21 |

Figure 9.5   Locations of areas activated prior (previous) and after (next) activation of BA 39–43 during the distinct experimental phases F, A and D.

of vote. These areas function, therefore, as hubs in the networks supporting decision-making. Connectivity of these areas is investigated by changing area subset boundaries in *Parameters* and studying the results in *Summary LORETA — Connectivity.* Figure 9.5 shows that these results for BA 18 — Cuneus, confirming that this area is preceded and succeeded by activation at innumerous cortical locations. Results for BA 7 — Postcentral Gyrus, 7 — Precuneus and 7 — Superior Parietal Lobule (codes 18–21) are also presented showing that these BA 7 areas are preceded and succeeded by a small number of areas in comparison to BA 18 — Cuneus. This confirms the role of this last area as a hub in the network supporting vote decision.

Rocha *et al.* (2010) showed that calculated $h(e_i)$ distribution has a power law pattern that characterizes scale-free and/or broad-range networks. Results in Figure 9.5 and those on source frequency distribution (*Amplitude Sources frequency and Band sources frequency*) corroborate this proposition.

You may study connectivity for other areas or group of cortical areas handling control parameters in spreadsheet *Parameters.* Change the significance threshold to check for data robustness.

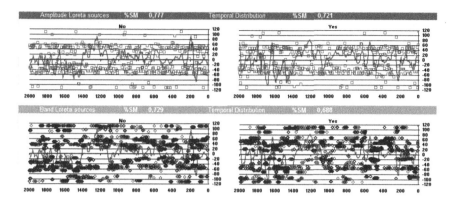

Figure 9.6 Superposition of ILS temporal distribution upon the *Grand Average* %SM — percentage of significant moments.

9.2.4 LORETA sources and grand average

It is possible to study the association between *Grand Averages* and ILSs obtained for the different types of vote when both amplitude and frequencies are considered. This may be done by superimposing the corresponding amplitude or band frequency ILS temporal evolution and the corresponding *Grand Average* as in spreadsheet *Summary LORETA* (Figure 9.6).

ILS temporal distribution shows that a large number of sources are activated during vote analysis. However, a careful inspection of Figure 9.6 shows that ILSs coded between 30 to 40 and 50 to 60 are active most of the time, in contrast, for example, to ILSs coded from 60 to 100 (see also Figure 9.7).

As discussed above, vote decision recruited scale-free neural networks having hub nodes that are heavily connected to other nodes in the net and whose function is to reduce cost of spreading information throughout the network. Areas BA 10 and 11 (coded from 30 to 40) and BA 18 and 19 (coded from 50 to 60) seem to play the role of hubs in the neural network recruited for vote decision, because they are continuously activated during the entire analyzed EEG epoch. Neurons at other cortical areas that are not continuously activated are supposed to enroll in solving specific subtasks of vote decision. For example, neurons at temporal and parietal cortices (e.g., ILSs

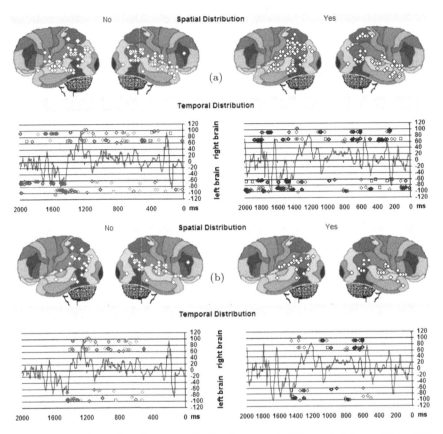

Figure 9.7 Spatial and temporal distribution of ILSs coded from 60 to 100 during the entire EEG epoch (A) and associated to W_2 and W_3 EEG components.

coded from 60 to 100) are proposed to be involved in calculating action adequateness and other intentions (Sections 4.8 and 4.9).

Willingness (or intention) of acting is computed by a complex neural system (see Section 3.8) that it was recruited for calculating vote intention (Rocha *et al.*, 2010). Figure 9.7a shows the spatial and temporal distribution of ILSs integrating this neural circuit, while Figure 9.7b highlights results calculated within time window from $-1,450$ to -500 ms corresponding to components W_2 and W_3. Results clearly show that both temporal and spatial location of neurons recruited by this neural system differ for Yes and No voters. This difference is very clear when the time window is restricted to components W_2 and

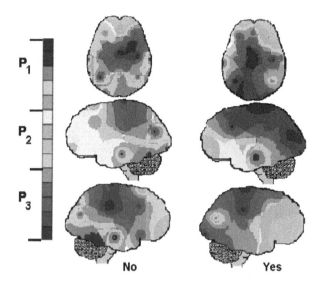

Figure 9.8 $h(e_i)$ mappings for No and Yes votes.

W_3 showing that intention associated to each type of vote resulted from different calculations.

Check for ILS temporal distribution difference for each of the other identified EEG components W_i by selecting the corresponding time windows in spreadsheet *Parameters*.

9.2.5 $h(e_i)$ and factor analysis

Mappings in Figure 9.8 (and in spreadsheet *Factor Mappings*) encode calculated mean $h(e_i)$ for each electrode and EEG epochs associated to No and Yes votes. Factor analysis (FA) identified three patterns of covariation that account for more than 70% of $h(e_i)$ covariation for both types of vote decision. Pattern P_1 is composed by electrodes F3, T3, T5, O1, OA, T5, T6 and O2 in No vote case and by T3, T4 and P4 in Yes vote case. Pattern P_2 is composed by electrodes FP1, FP2 and FZ case and by T3, T4 and P4 in Yes vote case. Pattern P_2 is composed by electrodes and by FP1, F3, FP2, F4 and F8 P4 in Yes vote case. Finally, deciding to vote No is associated with activity recorded by electrodes P4, F8, C3, C4, CZ, P3 and P4, whereas deciding to vote Yes involved electrodes F3, FZ, CZ, C4, P3, PZ,

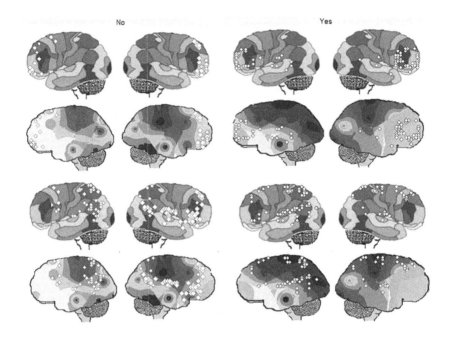

Figure 9.9   ILS associated with patterns P_2 and P_3.

O1, OZ and O2. These results show that besides recruiting neurons from different cortical areas, decision about each type of vote is also a result of different cerebral dynamics.

Contribution of each ILS to $v(e_i, t)$ recorded by each electrode e_i is dependent on the distance between the source and the recording electrode. Because of this, sources located nearest to the electrodes having high loading in each pattern P_i may be considered as contributing to the $h(e_i)$ covariation detected by each of these factors. Mappings in Figure 9.9 show that the ILSs nearest to electrodes loading in P_2 and P_3 No and Yes vote EEG epochs. By selecting area subset boundaries in spreadsheet *Parameters*, it is possible to generate these mappings in spreadsheet *Summary FA*.

Inspection of Figure 9.9 shows that ILSs contributing to pattern P_2 are mostly located at BA 10 and 11 (codes 30–40) for both types of vote, however their distribution over these BAs are very different for each type of vote. In the same line of reasoning, ILSs contributing to pattern P_3 are mostly located at temporal and parietal lobes (codes

60–105) for both kinds of vote, however their distributions are very different for each vote and mostly when right and left hemispheres are considered. It is interesting to remark that subset area boundaries for P_3 are the same used to obtain Figure 9.7, showing that this pattern probably discloses the neural circuit in charge of calculating vote intention.

Try to find ILSs that are correlated with pattern P_1 by changing area subset boundaries in *Parameters*. Are the results difficult to obtain? Is this because P_1 is composed by just to electrodes in case of Yes vote?

9.2.6 Multilinear regression analysis

Multilinear regression analysis was used to study the correlation between $h(e_i)$ and vote intention (spreadsheet *MRL-Vote*). It must be remembered that vote intention was described by means of seven different linguistic variables (see Table 9.1) that were recoded into values 1–7 to allow regression analysis to be used.

Inspection of Figure 9.10 (or spreadsheet *MRL-Vote*) reveals that high values of $h(e_i)$ calculated for electrodes FP2, F3, CZ, C4 and O1 are associated to vote Yes, whereas $h(e_i)$ calculated for electrodes FP1, FZ, F4, F8, C3, T3 and O2 are associated to vote No. Intention

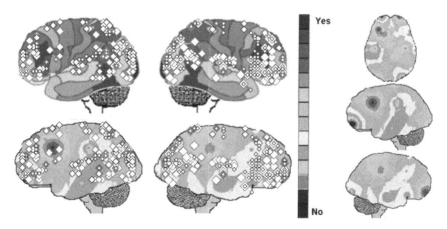

Figure 9.10 Multilinear regression analysis mappings as calculated in *MLR-Decision* and *MLR-Response time* spreadsheets.

to vote No was declared by 60% of the volunteers and the number of electrodes significantly contributing for this type decision is greater than the number of those contributing to Yes decision.

Check for the BAs contributing to each type of vote decision by changing area set boundaries in *Parameters*. Make a hypothesis to explain the results.

9.3 Brain Activity and Media Propaganda

This section focuses on the analysis of the EEG epochs associated understanding and evaluating media propaganda using data in *EEG_Marketing.xls*.

According to Rocha *et al.* (2014), media propaganda arguments to promote Yes and No votes had different ontological origins. Pro Yes arguments were based on empirical facts. Because of this, their analysis required recalling information from episodic memory in order to check argument trustiness. In contrast, Pro Yes arguments are supported by reasoning about personal versus collective rights, causes of criminality, etc. and logical coherence determines argument trustiness. Because of this, their analysis requires to use neural circuits supporting analytical reasoning.

The possible influence of a propaganda argument on vote decision depends on the supposed social threat being considered truth and important in Yes case or the alleged proposition being considered right and implying and important personal loss in No case (Rocha *et al.*, 2010). The veracity of the treat proposed by Yes arguments demands its probability being higher than zero, whereas logical coherence determines veracity in the case of No arguments. In this line of reasoning, highly probable believed Yes arguments would justify voting for firearm commerce control, while logically accepted No arguments would justify voting against the control. However, it is necessary to keep in mind that voters may have other reasons than those promoted by media propaganda, to decide how to vote.

Analysis of the 1,136 answers to poll questions about arguments used by media propaganda showed that half of people believed with arguments pro Yes vote and 76% of them considered arguments pro

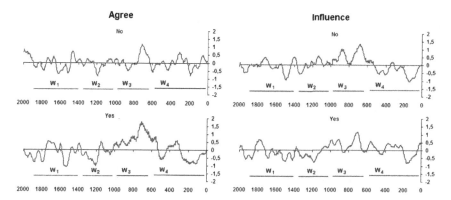

Figure 9.11 Grand Averages calculated for EEG epochs associated with media propaganda evaluation of arguments in favor of No and Yes voting as in spreadsheet *EEG Components*.

No vote as true. However, more than 64% of responders declared that media propaganda arguments would not influence their vote.

9.3.1 Averaged EEG

EEG epochs associated to evaluation of each type of argument (Yes or No) and each type of analysis (belief or influence) were averaged to be used for LORETA analysis and calculation of respective the grand averages (Figure 9.11 and spreadsheet *EEG components*).

Four EEG components (W_1–W_4) were identified for all types of argument and analysis from −1,900 to −1,400, −1,400 to −1,000, −1,000 to −500 and −500 to 0 ms (see yellow cells in the time window section of *Parameter*). Component W_2 is mostly characterized by a positive wave, while the others are mostly characterized by negative waves. Z score analysis shows that between 39 and 66% of the sampled EEG moments are significant at a threshold level of 2 (see percentage of significant moments in *EEG components*). A twofold increase in this threshold results in the reduction of 50% of these significant moments, stressing that the results are less robust than those observed in Section 9.2.1 for vote decision.

Correlation analysis showed no significant correlation between averaged EEG calculated for argument type or analysis.

Once the question about the argument (belief or influence) was understood, volunteer had to calculate arguments adequacy to promote corresponding vote and how much it may influence to their decisions, and based on these calculations to press the adequate decision button. Here, it is proposed that component W_1 is associated with question understanding and W_4 with decision button pressing.

Adequacy calculation requires evaluating if argument was empirically true or analytically consistent and to assess associated risk and benefit. Here, it is proposed that components W_2 and W_3 in belief averaged EEG correlate to these activities.

In the same line of reasoning, deciding about argument influence on voting requires to assess vote intention taking into consideration argument adequacy. Here, it is proposed that component W_2 in influence averaged EEG is associated with rehearsing calculated adequacy from memory and W_3 is related with intention calculation.

9.3.2   Activated cortical areas

Figure 9.12 (Spreadsheet *Amplitude Sources frequency*) shows the frequency histograms of ILSs location identified in the case of truth and influence analysis of media propaganda arguments, respectively.

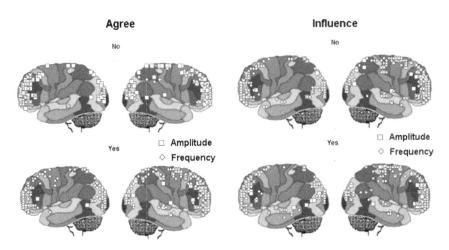

Figure 9.12   Frequency of amplitude ILSs identified as associated to argument analysis.

Inspection of graphics reveal differences on the frequency of the activated cortical areas activated by these analyses, mostly in the case of the most frequent ILSs located at superior frontal gyrus (BA 10 and 11) and BA 18 (cuneus and middle occipital gyrus) that play the role of hubs in the networks involved in analyzing veracity and vote influence of media argument.

In addition, ILS spatial distribution (Figure 9.13 and *Summary LORETA* spreadsheet) is different for No and Yes arguments, too, when both truth and influence are considered. In the first case, differences reflect a larger bilateral activation at BA 6, 7 and 8 and BA 7 and the right BA 19 for Yes in comparison to No arguments. Other difference is the activation of neurons at right BA 21 and 42 in Yes case.

ILS spatial distribution associated with influence analysis shows that bilateral activity at BA 20 and 21 and at right BA 39 and 40 predominates in Yes case compared to No case.

9.3.3 LORETA sources and grand average

It is possible to study the association between *Grand Averages* and ILSs obtained for the different analyses when both amplitude and frequencies are considered. This may be done by superimposing the corresponding amplitude or band frequency ILS temporal evolution and the corresponding *Grand Average* as in spreadsheets *Summary LORETA* and *Comparison* (Figures 9.14 and 9.15).

Figure 9.13 shows both spatial and temporal distributions of those ILSs, BA 10, 11 and 18 that are considered hubs in the networks recruited to calculate truth and vote influence of media propaganda arguments. Spatial distribution results stress those differences between analysis of arguments pro Yes and No vote are mostly dependent on ILSs located at the occipital gyri (Figure 9.13). In addition, temporal distribution results add evidence for hub role played by these ILSs since they were activated continuously during the 2 s of EEG analysis.

Figure 9.15 restricts the analysis above to those time windows defining EEG components W_2 and W_3.

Results obtained for W_2 time window show a clear difference between truth and influence analyses for both types of arguments

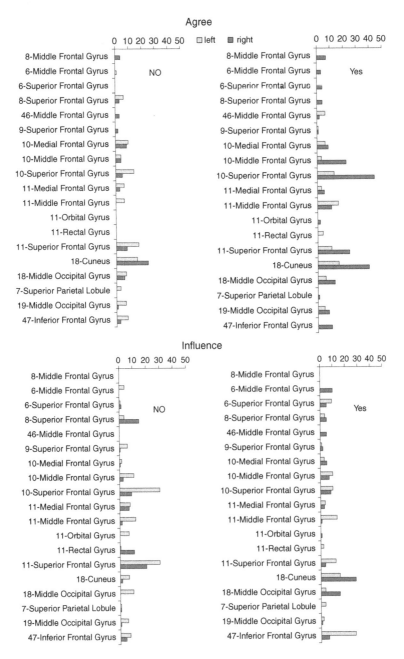

Figure 9.13 ILS spatial location as seen in *amplitude and band source mappings* and *Summary LORETA* spreadsheets.

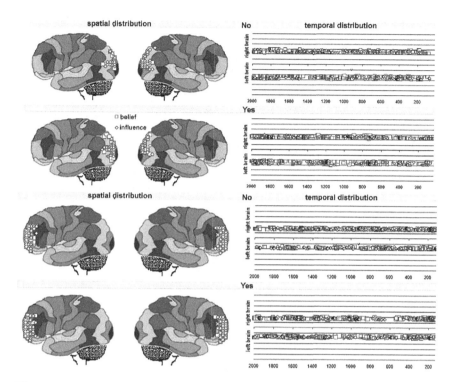

Figure 9.14 ILS temporal distribution at BA 10 and 11 (lower graphics) and BA 18 and 19 (upper graphics) that are considered hubs in the networks for media propaganda analysis.

characterized by predominance of ILSs located at BA 10 and 11 and associated with band frequency analysis over those associated with amplitude analysis (see graphics in *Summary LORETA*). In addition, it shows that band frequency ILSs predominated during the analysis of arguments pro Yes vote compared to those pro No vote, mostly in the case of influence calculation. One plausible hypothesis to explain these results would stress the role of memory to provide information about benefit and risk to be used for calculating vote intention supported by the argument proposed by media propaganda. Results also show that these computations are carried out during W_2 time window.

Results obtained for W_3 time window show that activity at BA 19 predominated for analysis of arguments pro Yes votes in comparison

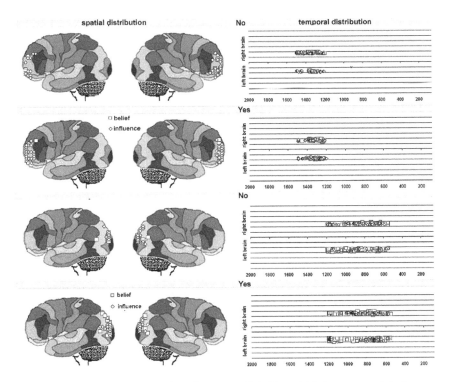

Figure 9.15   ILS temporal distribution at BA 18 and 19 (upper graphics) associated to EEG component W_2 and at BA 10 and 11 (lower graphics) associated to W_3.

to those pro No votes. One plausible hypothesis to explain these results is to consider that recalling data from episodic memory is more relevant analyzing Yes arguments in comparison to No arguments.

Check for ILS temporal distribution difference for each of the identified EEG components W_i by selecting the corresponding time windows and changing area subset boundaries in spreadsheet *Parameters*.

9.3.4 $h(e_i)$ and FA

Mappings in Figure 9.16 (and in spreadsheet *Factor Mappings*) encode calculated mean $h(e_i)$ for each electrode and EEG epochs

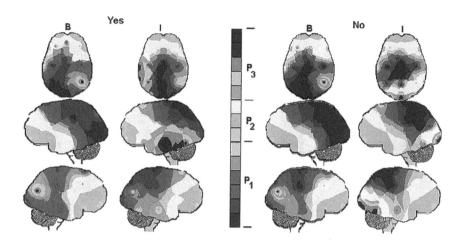

Figure 9.16 FA mappings for media campaign arguments.

associated to media propaganda analysis. FA identified three patterns of covariation that accounts for more than 60% of $h(e_i)$ covariation in the case of all analyses.

There is a striking similarity between FA mappings calculated for belief analysis for arguments in favor of both types of vote. Pattern P_1 in this mapping is the most simple one and its electrode P4 is the only one having a significant load in this factor. Pattern P_2 includes electrodes F3, FP1, FP2 and F8. Finally, pattern P_3 is the most complex one and includes electrodes F3, F4, C3, CZ, C4, F4, T5, P3, O1, O2 and OZ, and in the case of Yes arguments, it also included FZ.

In contrast, FA mappings calculated for influence analysis are different for arguments pro Yes votes in comparison to pro No votes. Pattern P_1 for Yes arguments included temporal electrodes, whereas that for No arguments is composed of the occipital electrodes. Pattern P_2 is composed by electrodes FP1 and FP2 for both types of arguments but does not include electrodes F3 and F4 in the case of No arguments. Finally, pattern P_3 is composed by electrodes C3, CZ, C4, P3 and PA for both arguments, but includes, in addition, electrodes O1, O2 and OZ in the case of Yes arguments.

Contribution of each ILS to $v(e_i, t)$ recorded by each electrode e_i is dependent on the distance between the source and the recording

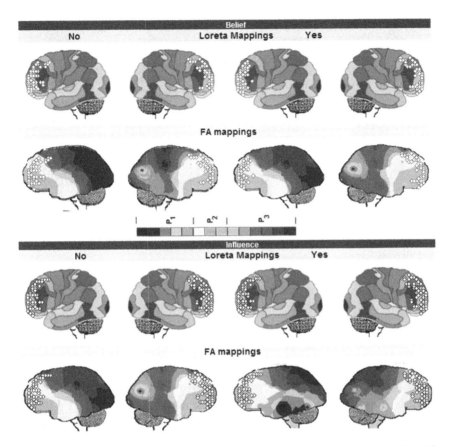

Figure 9.17 FA mappings and ILS spatial distribution associated with pattern P_2.

electrode. Because of this, sources located nearest to the electrodes having high loading in each pattern P_i may be considered as contributing to the $h(e_i)$ covariation detected by each of these factors. Mappings in Figures 9.17 and 9.18 show that the ILSs nearest to electrode loading in P_2 and P_3 media propaganda analysis, respectively. By selecting area subset boundaries in spreadsheet *Parameters*, it is possible to recreate these mappings in spreadsheet *Summary FA*.

Inspection of Figure 9.17 shows that pattern P_2 is associated to ILSs located at BA 8, 9, 10, 11, 45 and 46 for all kinds of arguments and argument analysis. Some neurons located at BA 10 and

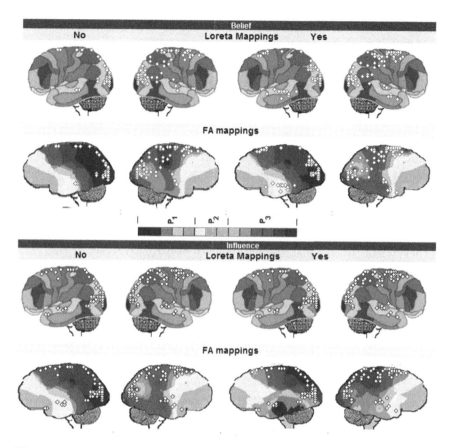

Figure 9.18 FA mappings and ILS spatial distribution associated with pattern P_3.

11 are in charge of analyzing value, benefit and risk (see Section 4.3.2) such that it is possible to propose that neurons in these areas are in charge of calculating trustiness, benefit and risk associated to each argument that will used to process argument adequacy to promote the intended vote and the influence of the argument over calculation of vote intention. Neurons located at BA 8 are described so as to be involved in estimation of amount of uncertainty in a given piece of information. Uncertainty about information carried out by the argument is influential over handling memory access in the attempt to reduce this uncertainty. Neurons at lateral BA 9 and 10, as well as

at BA 45 and 46 are proposed to be enrolled in working memory handling (see Section 4.3.3).

Pattern P_3 is associated to ILSs located at BA 5, 6, 7 and 8 that are reported to control attention and memory access (see Sections 4.3.4 and 4.3.5). Other neurons that are associated to P_3 are located at areas BA 19, 18 and 17 that are involved in storing information about episodic and semantic memories. Finally, neurons located at BA 21, 21, 37, 38 and 39 are proposed to be important in calculating adequacy and intention to act.

Data discussed in previous sections show that brain activity associated to analysis of media propaganda recruited distinct set of neurons when computing argument truth and influence on vote, as well as when arguments pro Yes and No are studied. Results in this section show that despite these differences, neurons are recruited to play two important functions disclosed by patterns P_2 and P_3 that are concerned to computing of value, risk, benefit and uncertainty, and to calculating adequacy and intention to act (vote), respectively.

References

Rocha, A.F., Rocha, F.T., Massad, E., Burattini, M.N. (2010). Neurodynamics of an election. *Brain Research*, 1351, 198–211.

Rocha, A.F., Massad, E., Rocha, F.T., Burattini, M.N. (2014). Brain and law: An EEG study of how we decide or not to implement a law. *Journal of Behavioral and Brain Science*. http://dx.doi.org/9.4236/jbbs.2014.412054.

Chapter 10

Multivariate Brain Signal Analysis

All the brain analyses described and investigated in this book require researchers to collect signals (or observations) of many sensors (or variables) to measure *in vivo* the cognitive activity in the human brain. In other words, brain data inherently include simultaneous measurements on several variables and consequently to understand the complexity of their information we have to disclose the relationships between these variables in a multivariate way. In this chapter, we present a number of mathematical concepts from linear algebra, information theory and feature extraction that are important within multivariate statistical analysis and have been applied throughout this book to generate whole brain mappings.

The chapter is organised in three parts. The first part, consisting of Sections 10.1 and 10.2, provides some definitions and results of linear algebra, more specifically matrix algebra, that have been used in the study of multivariate statistical analysis. A comprehensive exposition of these topics can be found in Strang (1988). The second part of the chapter, consisting of Sections 10.3 and 10.4, discusses briefly the idea of entropy as a quantitative measure of information, which leads to the electroencephalogram (EEG) summarization technique used in this book. For a broad treatment of information theory, the reader is referred to the book of Cover and Thomas (1991). In the third and final part, consisting of Sections 10.5–10.7, we describe in detail some feature extraction multivariate techniques relevant to formulate solutions to EEG whole brain mapping.

10.1   Vectors and Matrices

An array x of n real numbers $x_1, x_2, \ldots, x_n$ is called a vector, and it is written as

$$x = \begin{bmatrix} x_1 \\ x_2 \\ \vdots \\ x_n \end{bmatrix} \quad \text{or} \quad x^T = [x_1, x_2, \ldots, x_n], \qquad (10.1)$$

where X^T is its transpose.

A vector can be represented geometrically as a point in an n-dimensional space or a line in n dimensions with component (or coordinate) x_1 along the first axis, x_2 along the second axis,..., and x_n along the nth axis (Johnson and Wichern, 1998). In statistics, vectors are often referred as patterns and are used to represent the measurements of a number of variables.

A matrix is defined as a rectangular array of real numbers arranged in rows and columns. It is said to be square if it has as many rows as its columns. A particular square and diagonal matrix is the *identity* matrix I whose on-diagonal elements are 1s and all off-diagonal elements 0. The matrix I plays the same role in matrix multiplication as the number 1 does in ordinary multiplication (James, 1985). In other words, the following equation

$$I A = A I = A \qquad (10.2)$$

is valid for any matrix A of the appropriate size so that the multiplications can be performed. There are two other particular square matrices that are of special importance in multivariate statistical analysis: the *symmetric* and *orthogonal* matrices. A square $n \times n$ matrix A is called *symmetric* if

$$A = A^T. \qquad (10.3)$$

For example, covariance matrices are symmetric matrices. A real square matrix is said to be *orthogonal* if

$$A A^T = A^T A = I \quad \text{or} \quad A^{-1} = A^T \qquad (10.4)$$

and its columns are *orthonormal*. That is, for $A = [a_1, a_2, \ldots, a_n]$:

$$a_i^T a_j = \begin{cases} 1 & \text{for } i = j, \\ 0 & \text{for } i \neq j. \end{cases} \tag{10.5}$$

The eigenvector matrix of a covariance matrix is, for instance, an orthogonal matrix. It is important to mention that although a rectangular matrix can still have the property that $AA^T = I$ or $A^T A = I$, it cannot have both and, consequently, is said to be a semi-orthogonal matrix (Magnus and Neudecker, 1999).

10.2 Eigenvectors and Eigenvalues

One of the most important results of matrix algebra that finds application within multivariate statistics is the topic of eigenvectors and eigenvalues. We can describe the main idea of this linear transformation, often called the spectral decomposition of a matrix, as follows.

Let A be an $n \times n$ square matrix. The eigenvalues of A are defined as the roots of the following equation:

$$\det(A - \lambda I) = |A - \lambda I| = 0, \tag{10.6}$$

where I is the $n \times n$ identity matrix. Equation (10.6), which is called the characteristic equation (Magnus and Neudecker, 1999), has n roots. These roots can be complex numbers. Let λ be an eigenvalue of A. Then there exists a vector x such that

$$A_x = \lambda_x. \tag{10.7}$$

The vector x is called an eigenvector of A associated with the eigenvalue λ. Ordinarily, we normalize x so that it has length 1, that is, $x^T x = 1$.

In general, the vector A_x defined in Eq. (10.7) is a new vector that will not be simply related to x. That is, x changes direction when multiplied by A, so that A_x is not a multiple of x. This means that only certain special numbers λ are eigenvalues, and only certain special vectors x are eigenvectors. However, as pointed out by Strang (1988), if A were a multiple of the identity matrix, then no vector would change direction and all vectors would be eigenvectors.

Although eigenvalues are in general complex, the eigenvalues of a real symmetric matrix are always real (Magnus and Neudecker, 1999). This is a fundamental and remarkable result for the covariance matrices used here, because not only do the eigenvectors exist, but also there exists a complete set of n eigenvectors and their corresponding eigenvalues. In other words, there exist an orthogonal $n \times n$ matrix Φ whose columns are eigenvectors of the covariance matrix $\sum_x$ and a diagonal matrix Λ whose diagonal elements are the eigenvalues of $\sum_x$, such that

$$\Phi^T \sum_x \Phi = \Lambda. \tag{10.8}$$

Therefore, the linear transformation given by the eigenvectors matrix Φ diagonalizes the covariance matrix $\sum_x$ in the new coordinate system, creating a set of new variables

$$y = \Phi x \tag{10.9}$$

that are uncorrelated. In fact, as we will describe later in this chapter, this linear transformation essentially finds the principal components of the covariance structure.

10.3   Entropy and Information

Shannon (1948) introduced the mathematical foundations of information theory and the remarkable concept of entropy as an information measure in statistics. At that time, Shannon's original work on information theory was in direct response to the need for electrical engineers to design communication systems that are both efficient and reliable (Haykin, 1999).

Despite its practical origin, information theory, as it is known nowadays, is not only a deep mathematical theory concerned with the very essence of the communication process, but also a framework of study that provides a constructive criterion for setting up probability distributions on the basis of partial knowledge or limited information (Jaynes, 1982). This is essentially our main context of study here and, hence, the purpose of this section is to discuss the idea of entropy as a quantitative measure of information (Jaynes, 1957).

Let an event X have N possible values, that is, X is capable of assuming the discrete values $x_j (j = 1, 2, \ldots, N)$. Each one of these values x_j has $p(x_j)$ probability of occurrence with the two fundamental requirements that

$$0 \leq p(x_j) \leq 1 \quad \text{and} \quad \sum_{j=1}^{N} p(x_j) = 1. \qquad (10.10)$$

The amount of information gained after observing the event $X = x_j$ with probability $p(x_j)$ is defined by the following equation (Haykin, 1999):

$$I(x_j) = \ln \left(\frac{1}{p(x_j)} \right) = -\ln p(x_j). \qquad (10.11)$$

Equation (10.11) states basically that the amount of information described by the value x_j is related to the inverse of its probability of occurrence. In other words, if the N possible values for the event X occur with different probabilities and, in particular, the probability $p(x_j)$ is low, then there is more surprise and, consequently, more information when X takes the value x_j rather than another value $x_k (k = 1, 2, \ldots, N)$ with higher probability (Haykin, 1999).

The entropy $H(X)$ of the event X is defined as the expected value, or mean, of the information described in Eq. (10.11), such that

$$H(X) = E\{I(x_j)\} = \sum_{j=1}^{N} p(x_j) I(x_j) = -\sum_{j=1}^{N} p(x_j) \ln p(x_j). \quad (10.12)$$

In case any of the probabilities vanish, that is, $p(x_j) = 0$ for any $0 \leq j \leq N$, we use the fact that $\lim_{p(x) \to 0} p(x) \ln p(x) = 0$ to take $0 \ln 0$ to be (Duda *et al.*, 2001). Analogously, for a continuous n-dimensional random vector X_i, the entropy $h(X_i)$ is given by (Haykin, 1999)

$$h(X_i) = -\int_{-\infty}^{\infty} p(x) \ln p(x) \mathrm{d}x = -E\{\ln p(x)\}, \qquad (10.13)$$

where $x \equiv [x_1, x_2, \ldots, x_n]^T$ and $p(x)$ is the probability density function of X_i.

Equation (10.12), or equivalently Eq. (10.13), describes a quantity that increases with increasing uncertainty. As pointed out by

Jaynes (1957), this is an impressive result because not only is the entropy a unique and unambiguous criterion for the amount of uncertainty inherent in a discrete or continuous event, but it also agrees with our intuitive notions that a broad distribution represents more uncertainty than does a sharply peaked one.

In the discrete case, $H(X)$ is strictly non-negative and will be maximized when the distribution is uniform, i.e., all outcomes are equal likely. However, in the multivariate continuous case, the entropy $h(X_i)$ may be negative and its maximum value, among all continuous probability density functions having a given mean and covariance matrix for the random vector X_i, will be attained by the multivariate Gaussian distribution (Duda *et al.*, 2001).

10.4   EEG Summarization

EEG records the electrical field potentials generated by the activation of sets of neurons or source signals s_i located in several distinct cortical areas. The EEG data $d_i(t)$ recorded at a single electrode i represents a weighted linear sum of underlying source signals, that is,

$$d_i(t) = \sum_{i=l}^{k} w_i s_l(t). \tag{10.14}$$

The weights w_i are determined by the distance of the cortical source domains s_i from the electrode pair, the orientation of the cortical patch relative to the electrode pair locations and the electrical properties of intervening tissues. The number k of active sources is determined by the task being currently processed by the brain.

The statistical complexity of the investigation increases as the number of EEG and behavioral variables increase as well. Therefore, it is necessary to summarize the information provided by each electrode e_i about all sources s_i to make statistical analysis feasible and amenable. Since EEG data are assumed to be a weighted sum of the electrical activity of the different sources, correlation analysis of the EEG activity $d_i(t)$ recorded by the different electrodes may be used to calculate the entropy information $h(e_i)$ provided by each electrode e_i about all k involved sources s_i into a single variable (Foz *et al.*, 2002; Rocha *et al.*, 2005).

The rationality of this process can be briefly explained as follows. Given that data $d_i(t)$ and $d_j(t)$, furnished by two electrodes e_i and e_j, provide equivalent information about sources s_i then the absolute value of correlation coefficient $c_{i,j}$ calculated for $d_i(t)$ and $d_j(t)$ will approach 1, otherwise it will approach 0. The highest uncertainty about the information equivalence provided by e_i and e_j occurs when the correlation strength $c_{i,j}$ approaches 0.5.

Therefore, in the same line of reasoning used by Shannon (1948) to define the amount of information provided by a random variable, it is proposed that the *informational equivalence* $h(c_i, c_j)$ of $d_i(t)$ and $d_j(t)$ furnished by e_i and e_j is the expected value $E\{I(c_{i,j})\}$ of the information $I(c_{i,j})$ provide by $c_{i,j}$ (Foz *et al.*, 2002; Rocha *et al.*, 2004, 2005). However, because $c_{i,j}$ may theoretically assume values equal to zero, instead of using Shannon's logarithm function, the $h(c_{i,j})$ estimate has been calculated by

$$h(c_{i,j}) = E\{I(c_i, j)\} = -[c_{i,j} \log_2(c_{i,j}) + (1 - c_{i,j}) \log_2(1 - c_{i,j})]. \tag{10.15}$$

Now, given n electrodes and the average correlation coefficient

$$\bar{c} = \frac{\sum_{j=1}^{n-1} c_{i,j}}{n - 1}, \tag{10.16}$$

the *informational equivalence* measured by $\bar{c}_i$ can be written by the following formula:

$$h(\bar{c}_i) = -[\bar{c}_i \log_2(\bar{c}_i) + (1 - \bar{c}_i) \log_2(1 - \bar{c}_i)], \tag{10.17}$$

which calculates the information provided by $d_i(t)$ concerning that provided by all other $d_j(t)$. Thus,

$$h(e_i) = \sum_{j=1}^{n-1} [h(\bar{c}_i) - h(c_{i,j})] \tag{10.18}$$

computes the information provided by $d_i(t)$ recorded by e_i about the sources s_i. In short, in a cognitive task solving, we shall expect:

- if $c_{i,j} = 1$ for all e_j, then $\bar{c}_i = 1, h(c_{i,j}) = h(\bar{c}_i)$ for all e_j, and consequently $h(e_i) = 0$. This indicates that $d_i(t)$ and the corresponding e_i do not provide any additional information about the sources s_i;

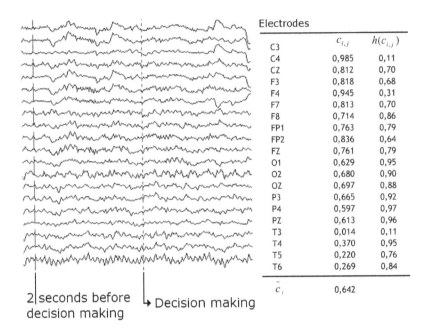

Electrodes	$c_{i,j}$	$h(c_{i,j})$
C3		
C4	0,985	0,11
CZ	0,812	0,70
F3	0,818	0,68
F4	0,945	0,31
F7	0,813	0,70
F8	0,714	0,86
FP1	0,763	0,79
FP2	0,836	0,64
FZ	0,761	0,79
O1	0,629	0,95
O2	0,680	0,90
OZ	0,697	0,88
P3	0,665	0,92
P4	0,597	0,97
PZ	0,613	0,96
T3	0,014	0,11
T4	0,370	0,95
T5	0,220	0,76
T6	0,269	0,84
$\bar{c}_i$	0,642	

2 seconds before decision making ↳ Decision making

Figure 10.1 An illustrative and hypothetical example of an EEG summarization calculated for the C3 electrode. All the calculations have been made using the previous 2 s immediately before the decision-making.

- if $c_{i,j} = 0$ for half of e_j and $c_{i,j} = 1$ for the other half, then $\bar{c}_i = 0.5, h(\bar{c}_i) = 1, h(c_{i,j}) = 0$ for all e_j, and consequently $h(e_i)$ is maximum and equal to 1. This indicates that $d_i(t)$ and the corresponding e_i discriminate two different groups of electrodes providing information about distinct groups of sources s_i;
- for all other conditions, i.e., $0 < h(e_i) < 1, h(e_i)$ quantifies the information provided by $d_i(t)$ about the sources s_i.

Figure 10.1 shows an illustrative and hypothetical example of an EEG summarization for the C3 electrode.

10.5 Principal Component Analysis

In most of the experiments carried out in this book, the neural oscillations that deviate from expected behavior are the information of interest. In other words, variance is a statistical measure that might be appropriately preserved in order to explain the dynamics of an underlying brain activation. This is one of the main reasons of using principal component analysis (PCA) here.

PCA is a feature extraction procedure concerned with explaining the covariance structure of a set of variables through a small number of linear combinations of these variables. It is a well-known statistical technique that has been used in several multivariate data analyses, especially for dimensionality reduction. A comprehensive description of this multivariate statistical method can be found in Fukunaga (1990) and Johnson and Wichern (1998).

In particular, let an $N \times n$ data matrix X be composed of N input observations (or signals) with n variables (or electrodes). This means that each column of matrix X represents, for example, the EEG summarization of a specific electrode observed all over the N observations and each line of it can be treated as a point in an n-dimensional signal space. The coordinates of this point represent the values of each variable of the signal and form a vector $x^T = [x_1, x_2, \ldots, x_n]$. For this representation to make sense in statistical feature extraction, we are assuming implicitly that two signals that are similar to each other correspond to two close points in the high-dimensional data space. For instance, Figure 10.2 shows a hypothetical example of a 2D signal space, where the observations are represented by triangles.

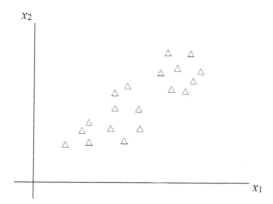

Figure 10.2 A hypothetical example of a two-dimensional (2D) signal space where the observations are represented by triangles.

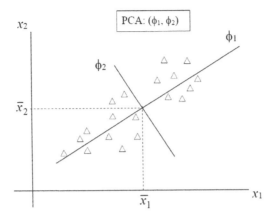

Figure 10.3 A hypothetical example of a 2D signal space, where the observations are represented by triangles and their principal components are the new dimensions ϕ_1 and ϕ_2 that explain the information that most deviate from the sample mean $\bar{x}$ described by its corresponding coordinates.

Let this data matrix X have covariance matrix S and spectral decomposition with respectively Φ and Λ eigenvector and eigenvalue matrices, as described in Eq. (10.8). It is a proven result that the set of $m(m \le n)$ eigenvectors of $\sum_x$, which corresponds to the m largest eigenvalues, minimizes the mean square reconstruction error over all choices of m orthonormal basis vectors (Fukunaga, 1990). Such a set of eigenvectors that defines a new uncorrelated coordinate system for the training set matrix X is known as the principal components. As illustrated in Figure 10.3, the eigenvectors are geometrically the new dimensions ϕ_1 and ϕ_2 that explain the information that most deviate from the sample mean $\bar{x}$ described by its corresponding coordinates.

Although n variables are required to reproduce the total variability (or information) of the sample X, much of this variability can be accounted for by a smaller number m of principal components (Johnson and Wichern, 1998). That is, the m principal components can then replace the initial n variables and the original data set, consisting of N measurements on n variables.

However, there is no definite answer to the common question of how many m principal components to retain in order to reduce the dimensionality of the original sample X (Johnson and Wichern, 1998). As pointed out by Fukunaga (1990), one useful property of such a linear transformation to consider is the effectiveness of each principal component. In terms of representing the total information of X, this effectiveness is determined by the magnitude of its corresponding eigenvalue (Fukunaga, 1990).

Although the absolute value of the eigenvalue of the spectral decomposition of the covariance matrix does not give adequate information for selection, the ratio of the eigenvalue to the summation of all eigenvalues expresses the percentage of the mean square reconstruction error introduced by eliminating the corresponding eigenvector or principal components (Fukunaga, 1990). Thus, it is possible to use as a criterion for eliminating or retaining the ith principal component the following ratio:

$$r_i = \frac{\lambda_i}{\sum_{j=1}^{n} \lambda_j} = \frac{\lambda_i}{\operatorname{tr}\left(\sum_x\right)} \le t, \qquad (10.19)$$

where t is a threshold value such that $0 \le t \le 1$, and the notation 'tr' denotes the trace of a matrix. For example, if we choose $t = 0.1$, then every eigenvalue which explains 10% or less of the total variance is eliminated.

10.6 Factor Analysis

The principal components described in the previous section can be named as *specific* factors in multivariate statistical analysis because their coefficients in absolute values indicate the contribution of each variable irrespective of the other variables. However, in problems like the ones under investigation in this book, it might be more appropriate to capture and interpret *common* information related to variation shared between variables and not uniquely measured from specific ones. This is one of the main reasons of using factor analysis (FA) here.

Analogous to PCA, FA, is a well-known multivariate statistical technique used to describe the association between variables in a non-supervised way. The main idea behind FA is to disclose the correlation relationships among the original variables using a few unobservable random ones, called common factors, to adequately represent the data (Johnson and Wichern, 1998). That is, in contrast to

PCA that attempts to represent as much as possible the diagonal elements (or variances) of the covariance matrix, FA aims at reproducing its off-diagonal elements (or covariances) (Jackson, 1991).

Again, let an $N \times n$ data matrix X be composed of N input observations (or signals) with n variables (or electrodes). Let this sample matrix X have sample correlation matrix R with, respectively, P and Λ eigenvector and eigenvalue matrices, i.e.,

$$P^T R P = \Lambda. \tag{10.20}$$

The spectral decomposition of the correlation matrix R of the data matrix X rather than its covariance matrix S is preferable because it guarantees that the variables will contribute equivalently to the total variation of the sample X and, as a consequence, to the computation of the principal components. The set P of eigenvectors scaled by the square root of the corresponding eigenvalues (Johnson and Wichern, 1998) and calculated as

$$\widehat{L} = \left[\sqrt{\lambda_1} p_1, \sqrt{\lambda_2} p_2, \ldots, \sqrt{\lambda_m} p_m \right] \tag{10.21}$$

is known as the factor loadings of the data matrix x estimated by the principal components method.

The estimated factor loadings $\widehat{L}$ of X can be rotated in order to improve the understanding and interpretation of the factors, especially if R deviates significantly from a diagonal matrix. If $\widehat{L}$ is $n \times m$ matrix of estimated factor loadings, then

$$\widehat{F} = \widehat{L} T \tag{10.22}$$

is an $n \times m$ matrix of rotated estimated factor loadings, where T is assumed to be an orthonormal $m \times m$ rotation matrix. Following the same previous hypothetical 2D example, geometrically we can understand T as the schematic rotations on ϕ_1 and ϕ_2 principal components illustrated as curved arrows in Figure 10.4.

Ideally, we would like to see a pattern of loadings where each subset of variables is highly represented by a single factor and has negligible coefficients on the remaining ones, allowing, for an example, an interpretation of the EEG brain mappings with no overlappings. Thus, our natural choice of the orthonormal matrix T has been based on the varimax criterion proposed by Kaiser (1958), which has been

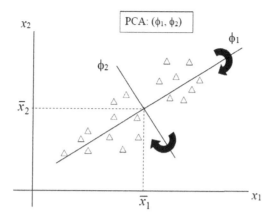

Figure 10.4 Schematic illustration of the rotation effect of matrix T, represented as curved arrows on the previously calculated principal components ϕ_1 and ϕ_2, used in FA to improve the understanding and interpretation of its factors.

followed by others in analogous works (Foz *et al.*, 2002; Rocha *et al.*, 2004, 2005, 2010, 2014).

Therefore, those $\widehat{F} = [\widehat{f}_1, \widehat{f}_2, \ldots, \widehat{f}_m]$ can then replace the initial n variables on m rotated common factor loadings, where the association between the variables would be not only the most expressive in terms of variance information, but also the most mutually exclusive ones given by the perpendicular rotation T of the initial factor loadings estimated by the principal components method.

A useful convention to determining an appropriate number m of interpretable factor loadings to retain, commonly encountered in packaged computer programs and adopted throughout this book, is to set m equal to the number of eigenvalues greater than 1.

10.7 Linear Discriminant Analysis

There are some problems that we might be interested in understanding not overall neural oscillations that deviate from expected behavior *within* the data sample, as described in the previous two feature extraction methods, but rather in disclosing variation *between* pre-defined (or pre-classified) data sample groups, as shown in Figure 10.5. Note that the previous hypothetical example now depicts

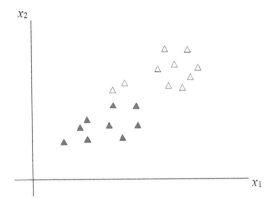

Figure 10.5 The previous hypothetical example of a 2D signal space where the observations are represented by triangles that now describe distinct sample groups pre-classified in dark and light gray colors.

two distinct sample groups of triangles represented by dark and light grey colors. In such situations, it would be more appropriate to capture multivariate information discriminated by a supervised spectral decomposition. This is the main idea of linear discriminant analysis, or simply LDA.

The primary purpose of LDA is to separate samples of distinct groups by maximizing their between-class separability, while minimizing their within-class variability. Let the between-class scatter matrix S_b be defined as

$$S_b = \sum_{i=1}^{g} N_i(x_i - \bar{x})(x_i - \bar{x})^T \tag{10.23}$$

and the within-class scatter matrix S_w be defined as

$$S_w = \sum_{i=1}^{g}(N_i - 1)S_i = \sum_{i=1}^{g}\sum_{j=1}^{N_i}(x_{i,j} - \bar{x}_i)(x_{i,j} - \bar{x}_i)^T, \tag{10.24}$$

where $x_{i,j}$ is the n-dimensional signal (or observation) j from class π_i, N_i is the number of observations from class π_i and g is the total number of classes or groups. The vector $\bar{x}_i$ and matrix S_i are, respectively, the unbiased sample mean and sample covariance matrix of class π_i (Fukunaga, 1990), as follows:

$$\bar{x}_i = \frac{1}{N_i} \sum_{j=1}^{N_i} x_{i,j}, \qquad (10.25)$$

$$S_i = \frac{1}{(N_i - 1)} \sum_{j=1}^{N_i} (x_{i,j} - \bar{x}_i)(x_{i,j} - \bar{x}_i)^T. \qquad (10.26)$$

The grand mean vector $\bar{x}$ is given by

$$\bar{x} = \frac{1}{N} \sum_{i=1}^{g} N_i \bar{x}_i = \frac{1}{N} \sum_{i=1}^{g} \sum_{j=1}^{N_i} x_{i,j}, \qquad (10.27)$$

where N is the total number of input signals, that is, $N = N_1 + N_2 + \cdots + N_g$.

The main objective of LDA is to find a projection matrix P_{lda} that maximizes the ratio of the determinant of the between-class scatter matrix to the determinant of the within-class scatter matrix (Fisher's criterion), that is,

$$P_{\text{lda}} = \arg\max_{p} \frac{|P^T S_b P|}{|P^T S_w P|}. \qquad (10.28)$$

Devijver and Kittler (1982) have shown that P_{lda} is in fact the solution of the following eigen system problem:

$$S_b P - S_w P \Lambda = 0. \qquad (10.29)$$

Multiplying both sides by S_w^{-1}, Eq. (10.29) can be rewritten as

$$S_w^{-1} s_b P - S_w^{-1} S_w P \Lambda = 0,$$

$$S_w^{-1} s_b P - P \Lambda = 0, \qquad (10.30)$$

$$(S_w^{-1} s_b) P = P \Lambda,$$

where P and Λ are, respectively, the eigenvectors and eigenvalues of $S_w^{-1} S_b$.

Therefore, Eq. (10.30) states that if S_w is a non-singular matrix, then the Fisher's criterion described in Eq. (10.28) is maximized when the projection matrix P_{lda} is composed of the eigenvectors of

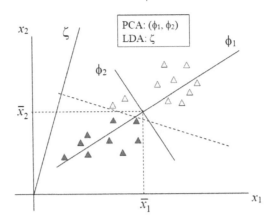

Figure 10.6   LDA and PCA dimensions of a hypothetical 2D signal space where the observations are represented by triangles that describe distinct sample groups pre-classified in dark and light gray colors.

$S_w^{-1}S_b$ with at most $(g-1)$ non-zero corresponding eigenvalues. Geometrically, recalling the illustrative hypothetical example of a 2D signal space, the LDA eigenvector ζ shown in Figure 10.6 describes the most discriminant projection that best separates linearly the distinct sample groups of triangles.

References

Cover, T.M., Thomas, J.A. (1991). *Elements of Information Theory.* Wiley, New York.

Devijver, P.A., Kittler, J. (1982). *Pattern Classification: A Statistical Approach.* Prentice Hall, Englewood Cliffs, New Jersey.

Duda, R.O., Hart, P.E., Stork, D.G. (2001). *Pattern Classification*, 2nd edition. John Wiley, New York.

Foz, F., Lucchine, F., Palmieri, S., Rocha, A., Rodella, E., Rondo, A., Cardoso, M., Ramazzini, P., Leite, C. (2002). Language plasticity revealed by electroencephalogram mapping. *Pediatric Neurology*, 26(2), 106–115.

Fukunaga, K. (1990). *Introduction to Statistical Pattern Recognition*, 2nd edition. Academic Press, Boston, MA.

Haykin, S. (1999). *Neural Networks: A Comprehensive Foundation*, 2nd edition. Prentice-Hall, New Jersey.

Jackson, J.E. (1991). *A User's Guide to Principal Components.* Wiley, Chichester.

James, M. (1985). *Classification Algorithms.* William Collins Sons & Co. Ltd, London.

Jaynes, E.T. (1957). Information theory and statistical mechanics. *Physical Review*, 106, 620–630.

Jaynes, E.T. (1982). On the rationale of maximum-entropy methods. *Proceedings of the IEEE*, 70, 939–952.

Johnson, R.A., Wichern, D.W. (1998). *Applied Multivariate Statistical Analysis*, 4th edition. Prentice-Hall, New Jersey.

Kaiser, H.F. (1958). The varimax criterion for analytic rotation in factor analysis. *Psychometrika*, 23, 187–200.

Magnus, J.R., Neudecker, H. (1999). *Matrix Differential Calculus with Applications in Statistics and Econometrics*, revised edition. John Wiley, Chichester, NY.

Rocha, A., Massad, E., Coutinho, F. (2004). Can the human brain do quantum computing? *Medical Hypotheses*, 63(5), 895–899.

Rocha, F.T., Rocha A.F., Massad, E., Menezes, R.X. (2005). Brain mappings of the arithmetic processing in children and adults. *Cognitive Brain Research*, 22, 359–372.

Rocha, A.F., Rocha, F.T., Massad, E., Burattini, M.N. (2010). Neurodynamics of an election. *Brain Research*, 1351, 198–211.

Rocha, F.T., Thomaz, C.E., Rocha, A.F., Massad, E. (2014). Brain mapping and interpretation of reading processing in children using EEG and multivariate statistical analysis. *Proceedings of the 27th SIBGRAPI, Conference on Graphics, Patterns and Images*. IEEE CS Press, pp. 251–258.

Shannon, C.E. (1948). A mathematical theory of communication. *The Bell System Technical Journal*, 27, 379–423.

Strang, G. (1988). *Linear Algebra and Its Applications*, 3rd edition. Harcourt Brace Jovanovich College Publishers, Orlando, FL.

Chapter 11

Concluding Remarks

Experimental data from electroencephalogram (EEG) studies in financial decision-making, dilemma judgment, voting and media propaganda understanding were presented and discussed in Chapters 7–9, respectively. Some general properties of cerebral processing involved in decision-making arise from these data and discussions.

Analysis of Grand Average calculated for 2 s prior to decision-making revealed the presence of four EEG components or waves and labeled here W_1–W_4. Although the format of these components varied according to the type of experiment, their time window was almost invariant: W_1 occurring in general between $-1,900$ to $-1,400$ ms; W_2 occurring in general between $-1,350$ to $-1,000$ ms; W_3 occurring in general between $-1,000$ to -600 ms and W_4 occurring in general between -500 to 0 ms. It may be proposed that each of these components is associated to the following general tasks that are performed to build decision-making:

(1) W_1-Decision identification: for example, choice of stock in financial decision-making (Chapter 7); action in moral dilemma judgment (Chapter 8); vote type in thinking about fire arm control (Chapter 9) and argument understanding in media propaganda (Chapter 9);

(2) W_2- and W_3-value, benefit and risk evaluations to calculate decision adequateness: for example, definition of quantity and price of stock to be traded; social and personal risk and benefit in moral dilemma judgment; social benefit and personal risk in vote decision, and coherence and veracity of media arguments;

(3) W_4-final decision about adequateness of decision: selling, buying or holding stocks; (un)appropriateness of action proposed as dilemma solution; certainty about vote decision, and media argument evaluation.

Low resolution tomography (LORETA) analysis showed that neurons widely located in the entire cortex are recruited to hand the many different tasks required for decision-making. A scale-free network is created by enrollment of these neurons to carry out decision-making. Neurons at some specific cortical areas such as BA 10 and 11 as well as BA 18 and 19 operate as hubs for access to neurons at other cortical areas, mostly those involved in

(1) information coherence analysis (e.g., BA 11),
(2) value, benefit and risk evaluation (e.g., BA 10),
(3) conflict and uncertainty (e.g., BA 32 and 8),
(4) attention control (e.g., BA 6 and 8),
(5) arithmetic calculations (e.g., BA 39 and 40),
(6) language processing (e.g., BA 21, 22, 37, 44 and 45),
(7) episodic and semantic memories (e.g., BA 7, 18, 19, 21, 41, 42, 43),
(8) working memory (e.g., BA 9, 10 and 46), etc.

Such organization reduces costs of spreading information in networks enrolling large number of agents specialized in handling the many subtasks required to solve a complex cognitive task.

Factor analysis (FA) and linear discriminant analysis (LDA) showed that neuronal activity in the recruited scale-free network is organized in 3–4 patterns of $h(e_i)$ covariation that are associated with

(a) pattern P_1 — Input data analysis: includes in general BA 18 and 19 and/or BA 21, 22 and 37,
(b) pattern P_2 — Processing organization and control: includes in general BA 7, 8, 9, 10, 46 and 47,
(c) pattern P_3 — Semantic analysis: includes in general BA 38, 49, 40, 41, 42, 43, 44 and 45.

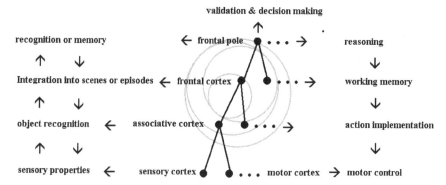

Figure 11.1 Schematic proposal for understanding cerebral dynamics of decision-making.

All these results support the hypothesis that neural activity related to decision-making has a complex dynamics (Figure 11.1) that involves many cycles (gray illustration) of calculations, coherence evaluation and summarizing results as evidenced by identification of at least 4 Grand Average EEG components; frequent enrollment of neurons located at some specific cortical areas (hub areas) and additional involvement of neurons located at other areas in charge of handling specific tasks. Specific patterns of $h(e_i)$ covariation are associated to this complex neuronal dynamics that are related to input data, semantic analysis and reasoning organization and control.

An important remark to be made here is that neuronal dynamics of decision-making is gender-sensitive, as observed in all experiments reported here.

Index

Printed in the United States
By Bookmasters